Falsified Antiquity

Thomas Hattemer

Falsified Antiquity

Slight corrections between 130 BC and 911 AD

Bibliografische Information der Deutschen Nationalbibliothek
Die Deutsche Nationalbibliothek verzeichnet diese Publikation
in der Deutschen Nationalbibliografie; detaillierte bibliografische
Daten sind im Internet über http://dnb.d-nb.de abrufbar.

© 2021 Thomas Hattemer
Covergestaltung, Herstellung und Verlag:
BoD - Books on Demand, Norderstedt
ISBN 978-3-7543-6212-9

Contents

First part – from my book 2013

The years 500 to 800 seemed illogical to me.
But if historian Dr. Illig is right, then that explains a lot.

Beginnings of Islam: 300 years earlier?

Almost 300 years are invented in the transition from ancient times to the Middle Ages – according to the art historian Dr. Heribert Illig from Gräfelfing near Munich.
Thus between the birth of Jesus Christ and the year 2000 not 2000 but only 1700 years would have passed.

The present book shows also Illig's astronomical calculations which support this assumption. On his innumerable explanations of archaeological kind in Europe is not to be gone into here any more.
However, the history of the early Islam and with it of the Arabs and Persians from the late antiquity to 911 is still unclear with him. Perhaps with Illig's theories also the decline of the high culture of the Majas in Central America around 1000 AD can be explained.

If I now accept Illig's phantom time from September 614 to August 911 AD as true, then further aspects arise for me. Because the history of Islam begins in the 7th century and appears credible, only the time before that would be invented.

When the Visigoths invaded northern Italy in 401 AD to conquer Rome 9 years later, i.e. 410 AD, the Arabs stormed Carthage in the same year 698 or 401 (698 minus 297 years). A militarily absolutely comprehensible thing.

The Huns are invented, the Vandals already destroyed at the Danube before 400 AD and the Visigoths only reach the river Ebro in northern Spain.

This book synchronizes on the basis of innumerable maps from the 3rd to 10th century the people movements, i.e. the military successes and failures of Romans, Teutons, Arabs, Persians, Vikings, Turks, Hungarians and other peoples and determines with astonishment how much fits together wonderfully, if the Islam was founded 297 years "earlier" (thus 325 AD) and on the 31.8.614 on the next day the 1.9.911 follows.

"Earlier" means: It is temporally correctly handed down from Islamic side, thus 622 AD However, the period from 614 to 911 AD does not exist on Christian side. According to Dr. Illig, Christian chroniclers manipulated history by artificially stretching Christian history by 297 years in a project that lasted until about 1000 AD. I and others suspect in order to be able to push Islamic history 297 years into the future, among other things. For the first time from 911 both religions couple chronologically correctly.

The history of the Arabs from 614 to 911 is shifted into the time from 317 to 614. Then everywhere in the world the period between 614 and 911 can be deleted.

The true-sounding story between 317 and 614 with the Persians must be seen anew from the perspective of the Arabs Islamized since 325. Between 614 and 911 the history of the Persians is apparently only passed down by Christian chroniclers. There all kinds of Persian rulers may be invented freely within these 297 years.
Islam in Persia was probably only introduced in the 10th century by a Persian tribe and not by the Arabs.

A new reason is given for the insertion of 297 years:

"It was about saving Christianity after 337 AD at Constantine's death." For what could be more embarrassing than when the first Christian emperor of Rome and his mother Helena declare Jerusalem to be the center of Christianity, and shortly after the emperor's death the city falls into the hands of the newly Islamized Arabs?

Forgery to strengthen Christianity against Islam had become necessary so that Scandinavians (Vikings, Normans) and Russians would not be converted to Islam by missionaries from Arabia, but would clearly convert to Christianity, around 614/911 AD At that time, Christianity was in dire straits. Arab raids were commonplace in southern France.

I think it is possible that the falsification of history was already prepared under the sons of Constantine the Great and implemented in Western Europe from Pope Gregory the Great around 600 to Pope Sylvester II around 1000 (there are 100 years then between the two popes – not 400). Dr. Illig writes in his books that probably under Pope Silvester II the phantom time was implemented.

The restoration of the original history has serious implications for the end of the Roman Empire, which had been largely different. Not Teutons and Huns but Arabs and Germanic tribes brought down the west of Rome in the 4th and 5th centuries.

Huge corrections are necessary:
(a) the Huns are pure invention and apparently attack Europe and Persia only to distract from the Islamized Arabs, (b) the Vandals are already destroyed at the Danube and sold as slaves also to Tunisia and (c) the Visigoths meet the Arabs in northern Spain and have no more possibility to penetrate into the interior of the Iberian peninsula.

Archaeology points to the correctness of these assumptions.

One finds no findings of the Huns, who allegedly came from Afghanistan. In Tunisia, shockingly little has turned up from the Vandals, so it may be jewelry from Roman slaves. Building activities south of the Catalan river Ebro by Europeans after the Romans do not exist until the 12th century.

Further the calendar falsifications are taken under the magnifying glass, which did not occur only since 614=911 after Chr. or 325 after Chr., but already 130 before (!) Christ had to begin, so that the time lie is perfected. 130 before Chr. means that the author has still another card in the sleeve, in order to support the time criticism of the Dr. Illig. Only unfortunately he did not want to take note of it himself.

In 130 or 129 BC a solar calendar was already introduced in Rome (however completely without leap years). The beginning of spring was on March 1, the beginning of the year at that time.

46 BC it was already shifted on 21. March.

The advocates of the official historiography and thus also defenders of Charlemagne set the beginning of spring March 21 to 325 AD at the Council of Nicaea. With Caesar the 24th of March would have been valid. Critical here is the year 1582, when 10 days were omitted to reset the beginning of spring from March 11 back to March 21. If one calculates more exactly, either the spring beginning 21. March is 46 before Chr. wrong and 325 AD correct or 297 years are freely invented between 46 before Chr. and 1582.

Overview of Illig's research and my ideas

1582: Change from Julian to Gregorian calendar: October 5th follows October 15th, which means: 10 days are left out. Heribert Illig: "But then only about 1300 years have passed since 46 BC, and not about 1600. Because then, according to the formula, 13 days should have been left out."

either

or

300 years are invented

in Caesar's time, spring began on March 24th (and not on the 21st)

Art historian Dr. Illig investigates Sept. 614 to Aug. 911 in Europe (north of the Mediterranean) as fictional

I suggest heir of Pergamon: 130 BC change from moon to solar calendar in Rome, with March 1st beginning of spring (without leap year). Then in 46 BC the 21st of March is beginning of spring. *But there is no proof, that Pergamon used a solar calen.*

Mr. Illig told me in 2004 something like that my idea "130 BC" has no historical basis.

I suggest for "south of the Mediterranean:" 317 to 614 is fictional. Dates Islam from 614 – 911 have to be pushed forward by 297 years to 317 – 614.
It must be carefully checked whether the years 317 to 614 can be deleted and replaced by 614 to 911.

Inconsistencies 600 years after Chr.

Chronology critic Anatoly Fomenko speaks of strange repetitions of history. The lives of rulers in phantom times like Illig's 614 to 911 are very similar to persons periods directly before or after.

For the family tree of the fictitious Carolingians is structured similarly to the real Merovingians. There are crises and climaxes of certain persons, which run quite similarly. The Lower Saxon Emperor Otto the Great is quite comparable to the fictional Charlemagne. Certain things from daily life in the times of the fictional Carolingians seem to be copied from the early Staufer period. On the one hand, Charlemagne is said to have revived antiquity, on the other hand, his subjects live around 800 in a more "modern" way (like around 1200) than the people in the (Lower) Saxon and Salian periods (until 1125).

Hans-Erdmann Korth wrote 2013 something about the annual rings of the trees in combination with the Carbon 14 and Carbon 12 ratio. There is a non-linearity for about 300 years. Adalbert Feltz from Austria also points out and adds that this is being ignored. More on that later.

Which honest person has then still desire to study history, if in such a highly technical world in the area of the history such a clog is dragged along: 300 years, which are not approached honestly, for reasons of the power politics.

We will see that around 600 AD it was only about Christianity gaining an advantage over Islam.

Which clear-thinking person now wants to see this advantage given up from the point of view of a Christian? The embarrassment before Islam would be simply too large.

Local history societies rave about the Lorsch Codex (Lorsch between Darmstadt and Heidelberg), where numerous village foundations are recorded around 700 to around 800.

Even if some villages are actually older and may have already existed at the time of Rome, if small settlements were mostly only "villa rustica". Astronomers hasten to emphasize that everything in the present historiography is in order.

Dr. Illig talks about archaeologically empty times: No architecture, no coin printing, etc. The art in 614 is identical to that of 911, an example being the ivory tablets from Byzantium depicting Christ or a ruler or empress. They exist in Ravenna of the 5th and 6th centuries as well as a gift from the Byzantine princess in Germany of the 10th century: a feigned standstill in art between these centuries.

In the school one gets finely taught that the 21st March was valid at Julius Caesar's time. If one calculates or asks deeper, then the officials want to have known nothing more of this combination "Roman ruler - day of the spring beginning". At present it is also worked on to shift the invasion of Alaric in Italy 401 AD by some years into the future, so happened in newer inaccurate historical atlases, in order to make the time synchronization with the conquest of Carthage by the Islamized Arabs in the same year 698 minus 297 equal 401 unrecognizable. But more about that later.

Because in the year 1582 AD with the change from the Julian to the Gregorian calendar 10 days were omitted, in the year 46 before Chr. the beginning of spring would have had to lie not on 21. March but on 24. March. On 21. March it would have been then only on the council of Nikia in the year 325 AD That 325 AD is valid, the officials claim now. The deniers of the period 614 to 911 AD continue to hold that 46 BC is when spring begins on the 21st.
Dr. Illig admits that on closer examination there is no proof that the beginning of spring in 46 BC is on March 21. Only why then one asserted this over centuries from the Middle Ages up to the modern times, as long as nobody recalculated

the 10 days 1582 more exactly? However, as will be seen in the following, there is some circumstantial evidence for March 21 in Caesar's time. Moreover, even the officials themselves claim that March 21 was valid in Byzantium and March 24 in Rome. What kind of confusion is this?

In order to clarify these inconsistencies, I make here crucial new beginnings:

1) Why is the beginning of spring on such a strange day as March 21 in the first place and not, for example, on March 1, 21 days earlier? Did the Romans introduce the solar calendar decades before 46 BC and make a mistake in switching?

2) Certain military procedures and peace settlements are completely illogical between 337 and 911 AD. If you let the Islamized Arabs loose on the Roman Empire 297 years earlier (and likewise the Vikings), you find, amazingly, how well the fall of the Roman Empire can be explained. One can save thousands of analyses.

3) Before the introduction of the leap year the year had 360 days, so (also) in the old Egypt. After four years the calendar was shifted in relation to the sun by 5+5+5+6=21 days. Again a reference to the 21st in Caesar's time!

The countless books that try to explain the mysterious fall of Rome in the present historiography become superfluous. Such inconsistencies already exist in the history of the ancient Egypt. There is even talk of extraterrestrials, because one cannot imagine that so far back in the past the pyramids could have been built. However, these buildings are not so far in the past. Similar buildings in Europe are supposedly younger and the trade goods that Egypt imported from Greece were produced centuries later in Greece in the first place. How does this fit together?

14

Mediterranean: North 614-911 South 317-614

Imagine you are an ancient monarch and a gifted general at that. Personally, I woke up in history at the attack of the Persians on the west coast of Asia Minor populated by Greeks and fell asleep again at the time of Diocletian. The rest does not interest me, for whatever reason.

Militarily it does not fit, if on the northern side of the Mediterranean between 317 and 614 massive war is led and on the southern, above all southeastern side around Egypt allegedly over 300 years (!) absolute peace prevails. This has never happened before in ancient times.

To me personally the time between 500 and 800 was strange and illogical and I could not make any sense of it, until I heard Dr. Illig speak on television for the first time in 1996 at night about 24:00 o'clock. However, I do not try to apply here the thinking of the Middle Ages as it does Mr. Dr. Illig, but I look at the situation from the position of an ancient man from best home and from the Mediterranean area.
It does not fit, if in the north the Teutons conquer the Roman empire and in the south the freshly islamized Arabs do it 300 years later. Above all, many of the attacks run synchronously over centuries, only shifted by exactly 297 years.
Nevertheless, one can be grateful to the time falsifiers who want to sell us Jesus on 2000 instead of 1700 years distance that they have preserved over 3 centuries the distance of 297 years again and again exactly, at least which concerns Rome and Arabia. With the Persians this looks somewhat more complicated.

What would be simpler then, than to push this officially shifted piece in the south by 297 years back into the past again on the northern piece on it, in order to restore the original state, so I ask the reader?

Both attacks, those of the Teutons and Arabs, proceed with the same speed, with the same vehemence, but above all with the same rhythm. The Teutons and the Arabs even cover approximately the same distances in certain decades: The Visigoths do this from Bulgaria via Italy to France and the Arabs do this from Egypt via Tunisia to Spain: Not 300 years apart, but simultaneously.

Because the years 614 to 911 north of the Mediterranean seem to be invented and the Arab history from 622 on seems to be credible, the history of the Arabs from 614 to 911 must be shifted to the time from 317 to 614. Thus the original state and also really taken place expiry would be restored. The deception has begun not only 614, but 337 AD at times of the family of Constantine.

The maps in the following chapter show that and how this transformation of the Arab history by 297 years back is possible. It is also necessary to understand why the Visigoths were never in Spain and the Vandals never in North Africa. The Huns are even completely invented. This applies both to the Huns who allegedly harassed the Germanic tribes and to those Huns who invaded Persia and served on both fronts only as a diversionary tactic of the time fakers from the Arabs.

Persian history, on the other hand, seems genuine from 317 to 614. Again, Greek and Christian scribes seem to have invented the period from 614 to 911. This is relatively easy, as the Persians - as far as I have read - did not have a consistent historiography until around AD 1000. I believe that I have read from the fact that in antiquity the Persian history was only recorded coherently by Greeks, Jews and Chinese, and later also passed down by the Romans. But I can be wrong.
When I heard from Mr. Dr. Illig 1996 in the television, I was enthusiastic about his equation of the years 614 and 911

AD (On the 31st August 614, a Saturday, follows the next day the 1st September 911, a Sunday).
Here follows a strategically important matter:
If the Islamic historiography is brought forward 297 years, then Islam arose in 325 at the same time as the Council of Nicaea. This has already been pointed out by the chronology critic Uwe Topper when he learned enthusiastically about the chronological discoveries of Mr. Illig.

And now comes my weakness for maps and history as well as power politics (Bellum Gallicum: Caesar does not lead his wars out of charity.):
My eyes opened when I got to read Caesar's Bellum Gallicum in 7th grade Latin class. To me, this man is a great realist. Christian writings are often strangely unworldly and incomprehensible. What do these people actually want? Are they covering up something clumsy?

When the Visigoths invaded northern Italy in 401 AD in order to conquer Rome 9 years later, i.e. 410 AD, Carthage fell into the hands of the Arabs in the same year 698 or 401 (i.e. 297 years later). A militarily absolutely comprehensible thing.
Only refuted (without justification!) this correctness in Wikipedia by our scientists. I hope I am also soon led in this list. Who has the power over pope and medieval nobility, needs no justification.

Galileo is no longer a problem for the Vatican. But that Charlemagne should be fictitious, that is then nevertheless too enormous. One would have to abolish Christianity to get through here. Galileo has many friends among the Nordic Christians. This does not harm them even. To abolish Charlemagne would harm them themselves.

17

Either I believe in no god, in one god, or in many gods. What does it matter! The main thing is that we all believe in the same thing. Perhaps in the future again in several gods.

It may be no coincidence that the first monastery foundations in Egypt in the 4th century AD are directly related to the invasion of the Arabs and thus Islam. It is precisely at this time that one hears a great deal of Christianity from the Nile.
Did Christian monasticism arise in Egypt because Christianity had to retreat into the desert before Islam around 340 AD? Did many of the monks at that time emigrate to Italy, northern Spain and France to found more monasteries there? We will see.
The first monk of Christianity is said to have been Anthony of Alexandria (+356). The Muslim Hasan al-Basri (642-728, so actually 345-431) expressed similar sentiments to Antony about his God-seeing: "If you knew what I know, you would weep much and laugh little." The two men could almost still have known each other personally.

The last ancient Egyptian mathematician, Pappos, lived around 300 AD This fits in with the fact that the Byzantines had to give up Egypt for good around 345 AD

Region/Year	0 - 317	317 - 614	614 - 911	911 - today
Europe			Illigs Phantom Time	
Arabia		Arabic Phantom Time?		

Region/Year	0 - 317	317 - 614	614 - 911	911 - today
Europe			Illigs Phantom Time	
Arabia			←	

A) Postpone the Arab events to 297 years earlier. B) Assuming that Byzantium or others invented the period 317 to 614 for Arabia, that can be overwritten. C) Then the entire block 614 to 911 in Europe AND Arabia can be deleted.

Year 1582: 10 days skipped instead of 13

The decisive astronomical calculation of Mr. Illig is the following:

In 1582 the Vatican skipped 10 days to let the beginning of spring fall again on March 21, as it did when the Julian calendar was introduced.
October 4 was followed the next day by October 15.
Now the Gregorian calendar is introduced, which is adapted more precisely to the actual year length of 365.2422 days.

Many Catholic states (e.g. German ecclesiastical electorates) followed suit a year later. Protestant and orthodox states suspected a plot or were not subject to the pope and followed only centuries later (e.g. German Protestants 1700, Russians only 1923), because they had to realize that the pope was right for once.

Since 46 BC (introduction of the Julian calendar) the beginning of spring had moved further and further to the beginning of March by the switching of too many leap years. It had already reached March 11 in the 16th century. One has inserted since 46 before Chr. every 4 years a leap day as 29th February, but exactly that is per century a three-quarter day too much.

To be able to calculate exactly in which intervals a 29th February must be added, one needs the exact year length in number of days with at least 4 decimal places.
That is 365.2422 days after precise astronomical investigations. One speaks here also of the tropical year which is decisive here.

The formula is then:

[number of days] = [number of years] times ([days per year in the Julian calendar] minus [days per year actually]).

The problem is, which is probably known to everyone who does the math:

If 10 days must be skipped in 1582, then exactly 1282 years have passed between 46 BC and 1582 AD, not 1582 minus (minus 46) equals 1628 years.

The numbers inserted and after the number of years dissolved results:

10 days / (365.25 minus 365.2422) days/year = 1282 years.

365.25 days/year is year length in the Julian calendar,
365.2425 days/year is used by Gregorian calendar from 1582 onwards
365.2422 days/year are in fact

That is a difference of 1628 minus 1282 equals 346 years! These about 346 years have not been lived through at first at all, but were added artificially in the Christian calendar. Or the beginning of spring was around 325 AD on the 21st of March.

With a tolerance of 9.51 to 10.49 days, the difference between 1582 and 46 BC can vary between about 1220 and about 1345 years. Thus, the fictitious years have a minimum extension of 283 and a maximum of 408 years.

This large tolerance arises because the beginning of the seasons is of course not exactly at 12:00 noon or 24:00 at night. It moves through the day always further, so that every four years a day must be switched, so that it can run again from new through the same day of the year.

If Dr. Illig determines now on the basis of archaeological, art-historical and political facts on 297 years the quantity of too much of years between 46 before Chr. and 1582 after Chr., then between these two corner points would have

1582 minus (minus 46) minus 297 = 1331 years

must have passed.

This means, by the way, a supplement of 10.38 days exactly. Because one can supplement only full days, it is rounded 10 days.

Although it is already nearly 10.5 days, something impractically was switched then nevertheless in the year 1600 because of the all-400-year rule: 1700, 1800 and 1900 have no 29th February, 1600 and 2000 however nevertheless. That means only that the beginning of spring lies three times on a 21st March and once on the 20th March, and just not once on the 22nd March.

To summarize it finally:

Only two possibilities are correct:

1. either the beginning of spring at Caesar's times was on 21. March & between 46 before Chr. and 1582 after Chr. are 1282 years (plus/minus 125 years)

2. or between 46 BC and 1582 AD 1628 years have passed & the beginning of spring in Caesar's time was on March 24.

In other words, you would have had to skip 13 days in 1582 to make it represent exactly the number of years between 46 BC and 1582 AD that it should have, purely mathematically.

The learning and teaching process then looks like this:

1.

in the school or astronomy courses one learns as a child:
Beginning of spring at Caesar's time on the 21st March.

2.

in the school or astronomy courses one learns as a youth:
1582 was skipped 10 days.

3.

both is taught so convincingly that one does not come at all
into the temptation to calculate, also not after university
graduation with the diploma in physics.

4.

some astronomers calculate perhaps and are silent.

5.

hardly an art historian recalculates, a light goes up to the
people who get to know him.

6.

the powerful fear the art historian and put the beginning of
spring March 21 on the council of Nicaea.

7.

According to this, the beginning of spring in Caesar's time
must have been on March 24.

8.

Even the art historian buckles and points out that there are
no documents about when the beginning of spring was in
Caesar's time.

Counter against phantom time

Although one learns in the school or in astronomy courses of his childhood that the 21st March was already at Julius Caesar's time the beginning of spring, one is taught with more exact inquiries with the defenders of the official chronology of a better. Everyone, which makes itself once the trouble to calculate the number of the years between 46 BC and 1582 AD, is then "enlightened", in Rome the beginning of spring would have fallen only with the council of Nikia 325 AD on 21. March. Then one must skip in October 1582 only 10 days and not 13 days.

It must have fallen then at times of Caesar on 24 March. Otherwise it is not possible. The beginning of spring is the beginning of spring! The day cannot have fallen at Caesar's times again on the 21st March.

However, according to Dr. Illig, there are differences between Eastern Rome (Byzantium) and Western Rome (Rome). In today's Istanbul, nevertheless, March 21 is said to have been the beginning of spring in Caesar's time. In western Rome it was March 24. At least that's what the defenders of the years 614 to 911 claim. How does that work together?

Exactly calculated result between 46 BC and 325 AD:

$$(325 + 46)\, years \, * \, (365.25 - 365.2422)\, days/year$$
$$= 2.89\, days$$

For the representatives of conventional historiography, it is impossible to coordinate such a phantom time over great distances such as between England and Egypt.

The monasteries were on their own. There would have been no networking.

I mean, does Byzantium have to destroy or rework stone inscriptions or things on paper? Is that necessary and possible? Constantine donation for the establishment of the Papal States is recognized as a forgery. But not 614 to 911 as a possible fraud.

Military history cards 337 to 1000

Let us consider the downfall of Rome through the conquests of the Teutons and Arabs in the 4th century (fictional 7th century) from the military side.

For this purpose, we draw the military movements of the 4th century north of the Mediterranean on maps of the Mediterranean (and Persia) at the same time as those of the fictitious 7th century to the south of the Mediterranean.
It is "making clear" as it could have been, even if in Islam the years 614 to 911 AD be deleted and Islam as early as 325 AD originated.
It's exhausting, but the end result will be relaxation.

I felt in Trier that something is wrong here, you have to feel it when you walk through the city, and then research ... and if you don't feel it, you won't accept the rational explanation ... .in Lorsch I thought the bars in the building were bending with lies.

The Roman Empire is united for the last time in its known size. Emperor Constantine, from Naissus in what is now Serbia, has an oversized statue erected to match his abundance of power. The foot alone is almost as long as a full-grown man. In any case, a statue of this size proves that everything here is still correct in relation to Arabia (still without Islam), chronologically. Without a potent Roman Empire, such a statue could not and would not have been financially raised for a single man.
The empire has only been missing the areas east of the Rhine, north of the Danube (occupied for about 200 years) and Mesopotamia (occupied for 2 years under Emperor Trajan from 115 to 117 AD) for decades.

At the death of Constantine, the kingdom is divided among his three sons.

24

And now the evil starts with the chronology.

The matter is not entirely trivial.

- The forgery was made public in the 1990s AD, and was probably discovered decades or centuries earlier.
- The basis is, among other things, the year 1582 because of the treacherous change from the Julian to the Gregorian calendar.
- The fairy tales of the phantom time were probably made between 600 and 1000 AD. (Charlemagne decorated until 1200 AD, locally in some cases even until 1600.)
- Calendar falsification goes back to the year 130 BC (theory 1 March beginning of spring).
- Between 130 BC and 337 AD, the actions are correctly transmitted militarily (and if you will: on the part of the migration of peoples).
- The acts between 337 and 614 AD are largely correctly passed down only on the northern side of the Mediterranean, except for Vandals, Spanish Visigoths and fictional Huns.
- The acts are between 634 and 911 AD only passed down largely correctly on the southern side of the Mediterranean, except that they actually belong to the period 337 to 614.
- Persia (apart from the Mediterranean region) is a special case.

Arabs (possibly supported by Persian auxiliaries) and Persians have only on the death of Constantine in 337 AD waited.

Shortly thereafter, the Arabs immediately invaded Palestine and Syria, with these Arabs in 325 (622) AD established Islam in response to the Council in Nicaea. In order to avoid becoming a citizen of Rome through Christianity and thus remaining free Arabs. The Persians, for their part, did not accept Islam for 300 years, but provided the Arabs with military support. It was not until around 930 that the Persians gave themselves a special form of Islam (Shiite) on their own.

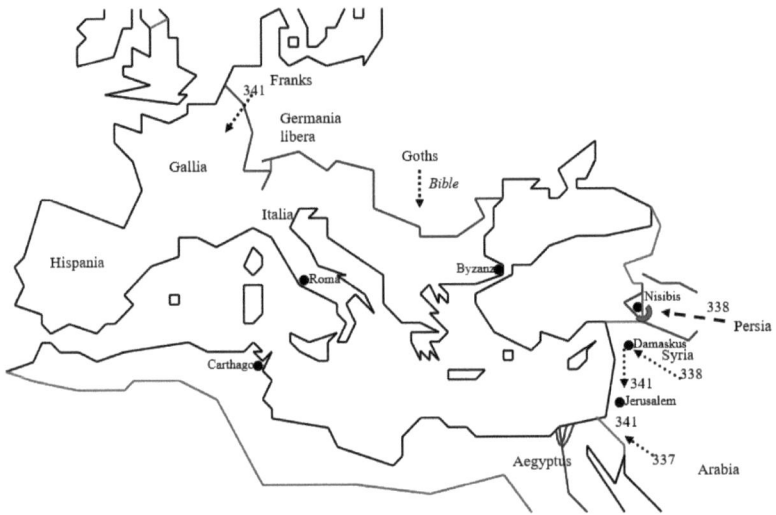

Arab-Persian incursion as well as Teutons 337 to 341 AD

The Arabs marched into southern Palestine as early as 337 and stormed the city of Damascus in 338, exactly 297 years earlier than the official historiography (originating in the early Middle Ages) pulled it apart.

In 338 the Persians besieged the city of Nisibis in southeastern Turkey as a diversion and flank protection for the Arabs. Only the Persian attack has been able to hold its own in official history; the Arab part was shifted 297 years into the future, into the so-called nonexistent period between 614 and 911.

After all, Jerusalem was Islamized by the Arabs as early as 341. What a blow to the Christian world after Constantine and his mother Helena had declared it to be the center of

Christianity only a few years earlier, and what an embarrassment. That smells like the need for time falsification. However, retrospectively only acutely in the greatest need for Christianity in 600 AD. From then on there are only 14 years left until the two contracts with the Vikings in Normandy and Ukraine.

The unrest in Palestine had an impact on the Germans who settled north of the Roman Empire. During these years the Franks invade Belgium from the Cologne area. In addition, the Roman Empire seems to be trying to form an alliance with the Goths who migrate to the borders of the Roman Empire on the lower Danube. They are converted to Christianity, facilitated by Bishop Ulfila's translation of the Bible.

In 342, a peace treaty with the Franks succeeds. This is sorely needed because in the same year Egypt, one of the Roman granaries, is attacked by the Arabs and is lost after a few years.

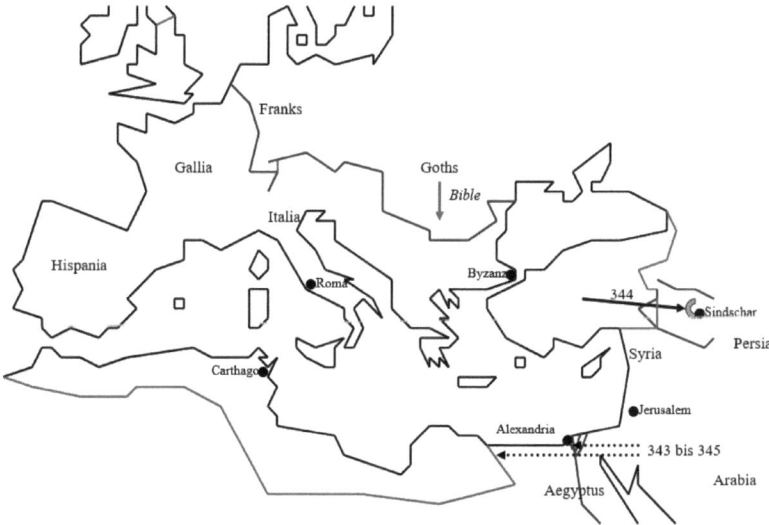

Arabs in Egypt and Rome against Persia in AD 342 to 345.

Islam finds its way into the lower Nile through battles between 342 (Heliopolis near Cairo, which was founded afterwards) and 345 (fall of Alexandria). The emperor in Byzantium was unable to defend the land of the pharaohs by sea, let alone by land. There is little support here from his two brothers in York and Rome. You have to do with the Scots and Teutons yourself. However, the Eastern Roman Emperor Constantius II succeeded in at least one relief attack against the city of Singara (Sinjar) in 344. It is not known whether Byzantium had hoped for a recovery of Syria or had firmly expected it. Because of the incursion into Egypt, the strength of the Arabs with regard to Syria could have weakened a little.

A little anecdote is that two columns were made in Egypt for the Byzantine hippodrome. While one of the columns could still be shipped to Byzantium in good time, the second column was only damaged and, due to the Arab attacks, it was difficult to get out of the Nile Delta. Today you can still see the pillars in Istanbul.

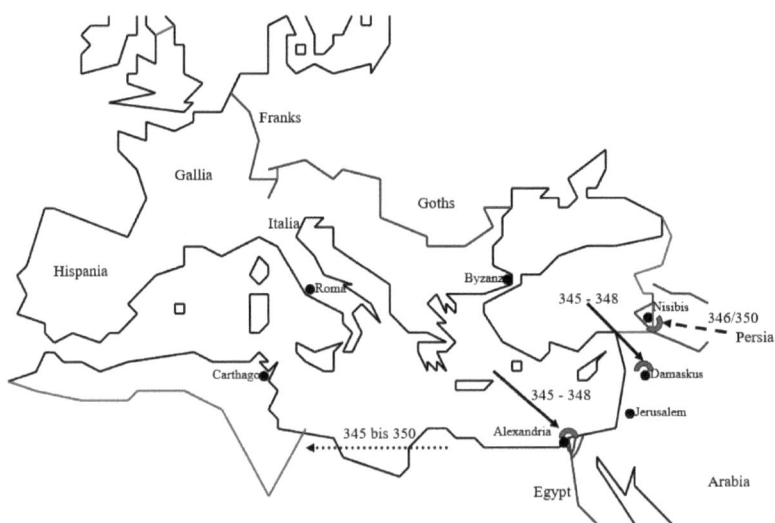

Libya, attempt at recovery, Persia 345 to 350 AD

While Islam continues to advance into Libya and overrun Tripoli in these years, the Byzantines can finally muster a counterattack by sea against Alexandria in Egypt and by land against Damascus in Syria. However, the attack attempts remained unsuccessful after fierce resistance from the Arabs. Also because the local population is on the side of the new rulers. After all, taxes were cut. The free Arabs from the Saudi Arabian Peninsula liberate the Arabs in the Roman province of Arabia and Palestine.

At the same time, the Persians try a second and a third time in 346 and 350 AD unsuccessfully wrest the city of Nisibis from the Byzantines. Arabia - in alliance with Persia - has meanwhile become a threat, especially for the Eastern Empire. In the middle of the 4th century it looks as if Byzantium is doomed before (!) Rome, especially since the pressure from peoples on the lower Danube such as Goths, later Bulgarians, will soon increase.

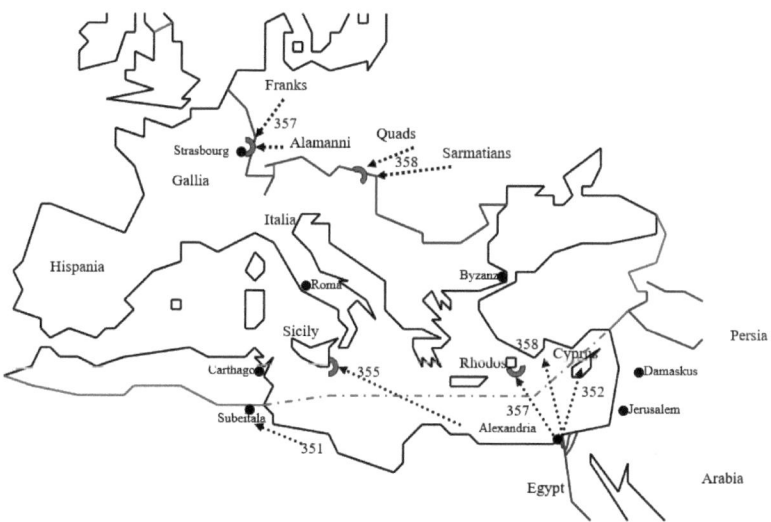

Unsuccessful attacks by Arabs and Teutons from 351 to 358 AD

The attacks on the Roman Empire are increasingly coordinated between Arabs and Teutons. Even so, these attacks are less successful than in previous years.

The naval fleet of the Arabs was built up by Phoenician marine engineers. She is now able to attack Roman islands in the Mediterranean. While Sicily and Rhodes are still mistaken for Rome, Islam can be changed in 352 AD gain a foothold in Cyprus. According to the sources, an agreement was reached with the Byzantines on a joint administration. It was only 300 years later, in the 10th century, that a Christian reconquest of Cyprus succeeded.

The coast off Antalya was hit in 358. A sea battle is taking place there. The sons of the desert reached the south of Tunisia as early as 351, presumably again with the support of Persian auxiliary troops. But it should take another 50 years before Carthage falls.
In northern Tunisia, Rome has concentrated massive troops because a fall of Carthage is an immediate threat to Rome, from the sea.
Officially, the Persians remain calm against Rome and Byzantium in this decade. The Alemanni and Franks were defeated by the Romans near Strasbourg in Alsace in 357, after they had invaded deep into Gallic territories. The Quads and Sarmatians threatened the Danube border near Vienna and Budapest in 358.

Now the Arabs seem to be giving themselves a break. At least in the 1960s. The Persians take the initiative and invade Asia Minor in 359. After a failed counterattack by the Romans on the capital Kteisiphon on the Tigris, the Persians were able to recapture the city of Nisibis after almost 100 years after the battle of Malatia. A strategically important point!

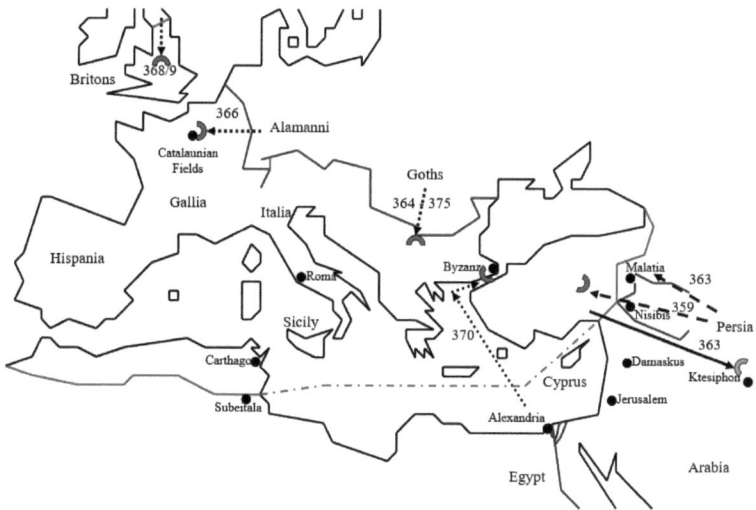

Joint attacks by Persians and Teutons from 359 to 370 AD

A year later, the Goths started moving south again and entered the empire via the Danube. After all, the Alemanni must be defeated near Paris, and there is tremendous rumbling on the British Isles. The Limes (Hadrian's Wall) is overrun by the Scots in 368 and the British struggle for freedom begins.

370 AD the Arabs pick up their sabers again and show themselves with their fleet for the first time directly in front of Byzantium.

Out of sheer necessity, Rome and Byzantium decide to win the Germanic peoples as allies as so often in the past (against Gauls or in the bodyguard). This time the Franks, Quads, Vandals and Goths must have from 371 AD. Arable land and pasture land (on Roman territory) are transferred. The local population is passed over by the government and has to come to terms with it. Probably even Romans settle in abandoned areas behind the front (Romanians).

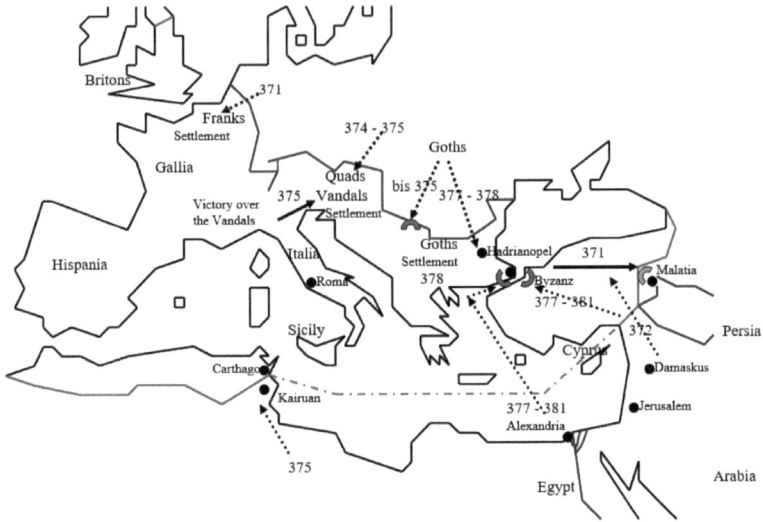

Arabs before Byzantium, Germanic tribes settled between 371 and 400 AD

On the other side of the Mediterranean, the onslaught on the ancient world is threatening its very existence. The Arabs advance a few kilometers to Carthage and found 375 the city of Kairuan (sounds like Cairo). Although no other areas have to be surrendered to Arabia or Persia, that does not mean that there will not be massive attacks on Roman traders and merchants.

While the Teutons break through the borders in the north and settle on Roman soil, the city of Byzantium is exposed to constant bombardment. While the Romans tried to retake the area around Nisibis in 371, Arabia started a counterattack in 372 and invaded Asia Minor. Between 377 and 381 there was the first threatening siege of Byzantium by the Islamized Arabs, both by sea and by land. According to official sources, the Persians limit themselves to a pure defensive stance. But presumably they were heavily involved in the siege of Byzantium.

In 375 the vandals were defeated on the Danube near Vienna. That they are said to have crossed the Rhine near Mainz from 406 and moved to Spain and Tunisia is an old wives' tale. 375 is its final end. Elegant vandals are sometimes sold as far as Carthage. Hence the jewelry that you will find there. There are hardly any traces there, only easily transportable Germanic objects. The official historiography speaks of the takeover of the Roman infrastructure (buildings, streets).

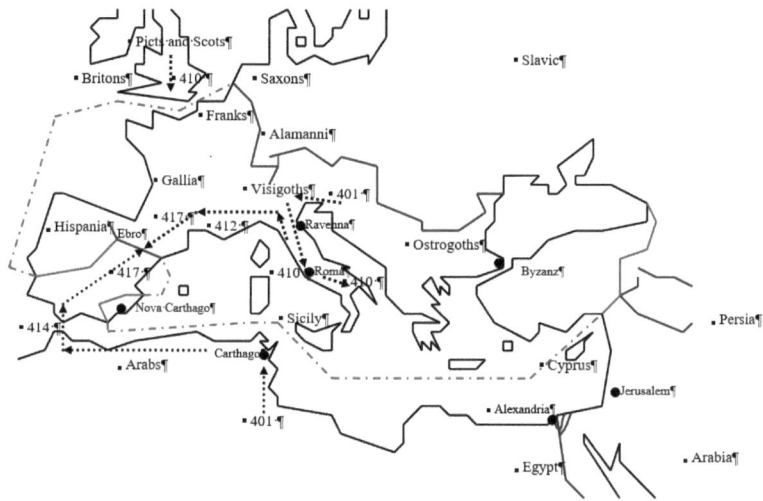

401 AD Carthage and Northern Italy / to 417 Western Rome's downfall

The year 401 AD is probably the most important clue from a military-strategic point of view for the simultaneity of the Arab-Germanic attacks on the Roman Empire.

If one subtracts from the fall of Carthage to the Arabs in 698 AD 297 years, you get to the year 401 AD. Exactly in this year the Visigoths invade northern Italy under Alaric.
The Romans have to protect their own homeland and completely give up Tunisia. That sounds all too logical. An

important synchronization and restoration of the real time for the southern Mediterranean is this.

Thirdly, in exactly this year 401 in Britain, the natives push the Roman state power into the extreme south of the island.

The dominance of the rulers in Byzantium over those in Rome leads after 401 AD with the fact that now not the east, but the west collapses dramatically, although it looked different at first. The Greeks' revenge for submission to Rome? Rome is conquered and sacked by the Visigoths in 410. 750 years ago the city was last open to the Gauls under Brennus. Those were very different times.

The Visigoths now move beyond Rome to southern Italy. In the same year their leader Alarich dies before the planned crossing to North Africa in Cosenza. So he wanted to break into the Arab front, right on the heights of Carthage.
Attacking Islam at Carthage is too risky for his successor, Athaulf. Meanwhile, he marries the imprisoned sister of Emperor Honorius, Galla Placida. Honorius himself received twice the counter-emperor Attalus Priscus 410/411 and 414/415 from the Visigoths.

As early as 412, the Visigoths withdrew from Italy, leaving Provence in the south of France behind and settling in Aquitaine with the cities of Toulouse and Bordeaux. After Athaulf's death in 415, his brother Wallia founded the empire of Tolosa in southern France. The Visigoths thus form a bulwark against the Arabs, who will sail through the Strait of Gibraltar in 414.

With the fall of Carthage, the Arabs suspend their 50-year pause from conquest and quickly move on to the west. In 414 they cross over to Spain near Gibraltar and in 417 they reach the river Ebro in northern Spain (near Barcelona).

There they meet the concentrated armed forces of Romans and Teutons.

Only the area south of Alicante near New Carthage can hold out until 459 (plus 297 equals 756). The north of the Iberian Peninsula should never be conquered by the Arabs. Centuries earlier, the Romans also had trouble conquering northwestern Spain. Difficult to access, economically remote and littered with wild mountain people.

According to the author, it is not entirely clear whether the Arabs will cross the Ebro this year or later. Perhaps Charlemagne will be allowed to recapture the small stretch from southern France to the Ebro as an invented bonus. Perhaps the Arabs never got beyond the Ebro.

As early as 410 - when Rome and Italy (with the exception of Ravenna) fell - the Romans were finally driven from the British Isles.

In the years from 418 to 449, the Roman Empire was largely able to hold its borders. Against the enemy from the south, one maintains a defensive position. The enemy from the north, with whom one is always allied and who has not yet touched the imperial frontier there (with the exception of Britain), is settling more and more numerous, bolder and more self-confident on imperial territory. While the Burgundians 406 only come across the Rhine near Worms, they have already built up settlements in 443 in Burgundy / France. A joint armed conflict between the Franks and Romans drove them there. Visigoths, Ostrogoths and Franks make themselves comfortable in Gaul and the Balkans.

The Gallo-Roman bishop Sidonius Apollinaris from Auvergne complains in his letters to the relatives about the hygienic conditions among the Teutons.

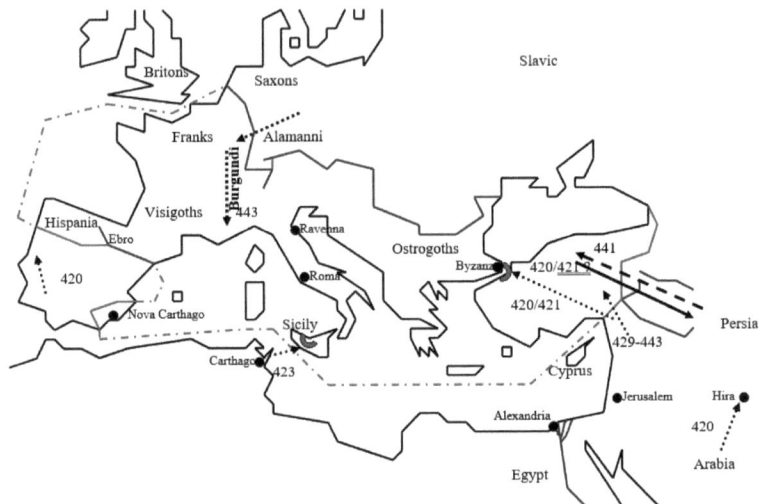

Rome and Byzantium under siege, until 449 AD

Fighting (as long as allied with the Teutons) is mainly in Spain, Asia Minor and Sicily against Arabs and Persians. On the Iberian Peninsula, what is now Portugal comes completely under Islamic rule. Sicily was attacked again in 423 without success. Asia Minor becomes a marching area on the way to Byzantium and during this time it was exposed to the Arab and Persian military for more than 20 years.

The areas north of the Danube deserted by the Teutons are gradually becoming interesting for multitudes from the east, but also for people from the Roman Empire.

At 420 (plus 297 equals to "around" 720) we have the first case of unfriendly Arab interference in Persia, in the form of the city of Hira on the Euphrates. An Arab tribe populates this Iraqi area, which was previously under the Persian Sassanids.

What actually happened between Arabia and Persia in the early stages of Islam?

Arabia is turned towards Islam, Persia still the old faith. Almost 100 years between 337 and 420 AD are both successful allies against Rome and Byzantium.

Now the advance of the Arabs is slowly coming to a standstill, and the question may be asked whether these two partners will still be in agreement in the future.

Because how does Islam come to Persia if history has to be rewritten "a little" because of the missing years between 614 and 911?

There are several options here for Islam:

a) The conquest of North Africa and Persia took place at the same time.
b) The conquest of North Africa must be accounted for with "minus 297 years". Islam in Persia arose independently and "voluntarily" because of the implementation of the Persian court ceremonial and the special direction "Shiites" (in contrast to the Sunnis among the Arabs). The Islamization of Persia must therefore be accounted for with "plus 297 years".

However, the author has excluded case a). Because 1. the fall of Carthage fits too well with the invasion of the Visigoths in northern Italy in 401 AD and 2. the Persian kings (from the Sassanid family) are too credible until their end in the 10th century (= 7th century), if only because of their huge graves in the rock walls. At most it could be that the last representatives of this family did not exist. But if this can also be denied, then why should the successors of the Sassanids (such as the Bujids from northern Iraq around Tehran) still claim the title "King of Kings" at the end of the 10th century if they do not as successors of the Sassanids to do.

From b) it follows that

1. all annual dates of the Arab conquest in North Africa not e.g. 698 AD, but 401 AD took place, and not AD 634, but AD 337. etc. From b) it also follows that
2. all annual dates of the Islamization of Persia not e.g. 633 or 651 AD, but (roughly) 930 or 948 AD have taken place.

I assume that the conquest of North Africa (also because of the Persian architectural styles in Spain) was not accomplished solely by the Islamized Arabs, but with Persian auxiliary troops. Dr. Illig refers to these architectural styles of the Persian type.

Even if Arabs (like so many other peoples at other times) invade Persia or settle there as peaceful "guest workers", it seems because of the Persian tribe of the Bujids that the Persians themselves have prescribed Islam, and only in the 10th century.
The famous Persian poet Fersaudi does not even mention Islam in his poem from the end of the 10th century to his sultan, according to a reference by Dr. Illig.
Following the introduction of Islam, followers of Zarathrusta's teachings emigrated to India.

So before we go on with the Mediterranean maps, I would like to take this opportunity to offer the reader a map of Persia.
The conquests of the Persian Bujids in the 10th century almost coincides with the apparent conquests of the Arabs in the 7th century, i.e. 297 years earlier in the phantom time. It can therefore be assumed, and here I will certainly again be neatly refuted by the established historians, that the Arabs did not conquer Persia at all.

In the next two maps we will see that the Arabs cannot attack the present-day area of Persia, but that they are permanently settling in the middle of present-day Iraq (Mesopotamia).

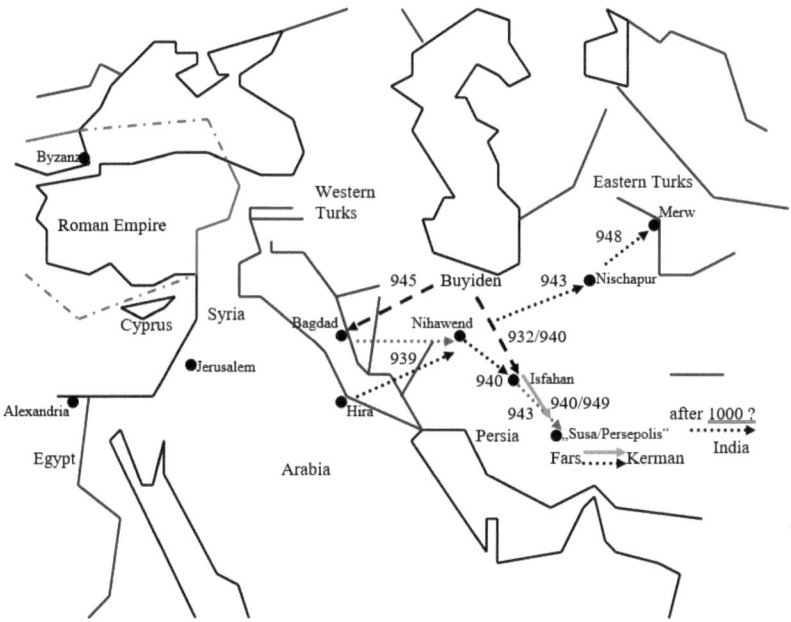

Arab, actually Bujidic conquests 932 to 949 AD?

In the map there are apparently Arab conquests around 297 years from e.g. 642 to 939 AD has been relocated to the future. They then coincide almost exactly with those of the Buyids not only geographically, but also in terms of time.
After we have agreed on this kind of Islamization of Persia, now back to the development in the Mediterranean area.

So we have to jump back from the 10th century to the 5th century!
In between are not five, but only two centuries!

The situation between 450 and 480 AD looks like on the following card:

The Roman world between 450 and 480 AD

As already mentioned, the focus of the Arabs shifts to the Persians due to the fact that they can no longer advance on Roman territory. In the course of the re-establishment of Baghdad in 465 by the Arabs on Persian territory, their capital Kteisophon (now in Iraq) could have been destroyed at the same time. That is not certain, but it would be plausible. The Arabs move from Hira on the Euphrates to Kteisophon (formerly Seulekia) on the Tigris, destroy the city (the remains of the Sassanid palace are still clearly visible today) and establish Baghdad north of it on the Tigris.

With the capture of "Nova Carthage" in Spain 459, the entire center and the entire south of the Iberian Peninsula are now in Arab hands. The ancient city of Cordoba becomes the seat of the Caliphate in the same year 459. Officially, both took place in the year 756.

The city of Rome is attacked [not by the Vandals, but] by the Arabs from Tunis in 455. The Romans repel the attack. If the attack took place at all, it would be possible.

Britain receives visits from Anglers, Jutes and Saxons from Denmark and Northern Germany from around 450 AD. The Roman fleet has withdrawn and so the northern peoples have free rein again. The first Viking raid on England, more precisely on Lindisfarne Monastery, took place in 496.

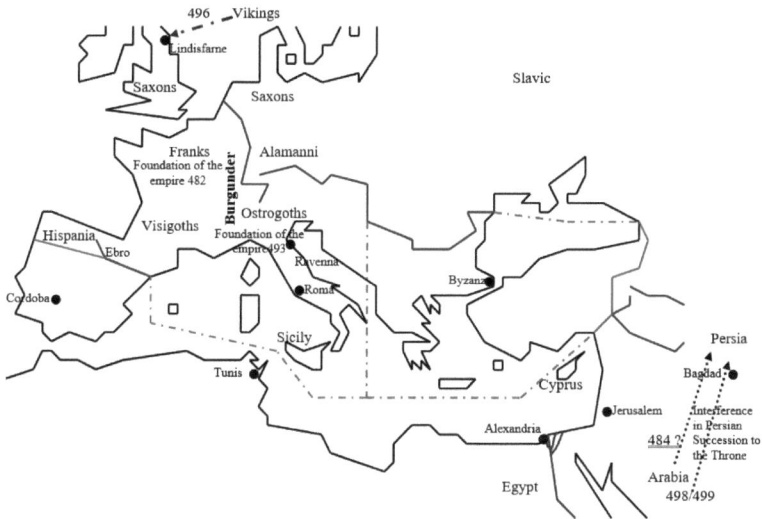

Germanic Empires, Persia, Vikings AD 480 to 500.

The Western Roman Empire was founded in AD 476. dissolved by the Gepids Odoacer. Byzantium had sent a few mock emperors to Rome. Now Byzantium tries to influence the Germans in Italy through the Pope in Rome. The Franks and Ostrogoths as well as other Germanic peoples founded their empires on formerly western Roman territory, 482 the Franks in Gaul, 493 the Ostrogoths in northern Italy.

41

Officially, the non-existent Huns interfere in the Persian line of succession. As with the Teutons and Romans, the Huns are also supposed to distract those interested in history from the Arabs by 297 years with the Persians.

The date of the apparently Hunnish interference in Persia - according to Greek historians of that time - can be ideally interpreted as a clue for the first strong pressure of Islam on Persia. In 484 and 498/499, the Arabs from the south (and not the fictional Huns from the north) interfered in the Persian controversy for the throne.

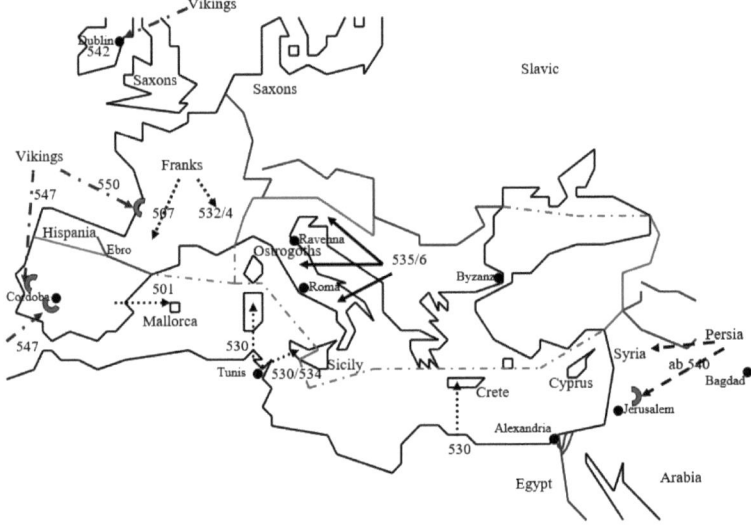

The world out of joint: 500 to 550 AD

Basically, it's not that wrong, the Middle Ages with the year 500 AD to get started. The ancient world is now completely out of joint and is suffering irreparable damage.

In the entire Mediterranean area, the ancient world is being "plowed under" by many different powers. The Constantine family comes from what is now Serbia. People seem to have a gift for ending ages and starting new ones. In 1914 they finally decided to leave behind the Middle Ages, which the European nobility longed for in the 19th century.

We count on:

- 501 AD: Arabs conquer the Balearic Islands and with them Mallorca.
- 507 AD: Franks destroy the Visigothic empire in Aquitaine (cities: Bordeaux, Toulouse).
- 530 AD: Arabs completely occupy Sardinia and Crete and secure bases in eastern Sicily.
- 532 to 534 AD: Franks destroy the Burgundy empire.
- 534 AD: Arabs expand their position in eastern Sicily.
- 535 and 536 AD: Byzantines inherit the Ostrogoth Empire in Italy. In the period that followed, magnificent buildings were built in Ravenna under Emperor Justinian and Empress Theodora.
- from 540 AD: Under a new strong ruler, the Persians try to break away from Arab influence (especially in the west of their domain). They invade Syria and lay siege to Jerusalem.
- 542 AD: Vikings attack Ireland for the first time.
- 547 AD: Vikings haunt the west Iberian coasts and reach the Arabian Cordoba in Spain.
- 550 AD: Vikings attack the Franconian Bordeaux.

It is certainly also a fairy tale that Byzantium recaptured large parts of the western Mediterranean in the 6th century, with General Belisarius and Admiral Narses. This fairy tale is set up so that the Arabs not only in 401, but also in the fictional year 698 AD meet Roman associations in Tunisia.

For the Arabs, it does not matter whether they encounter Western or Eastern Roman units there, they simply speak of the "Romans" in the Koran. Byzantine possessions are falsified in three places because it is correct:

1. Italy is not taken militarily.
2. Southern Spain and western North Africa are not occupied.
3. Egypt and Palestine are long lost (200 years ago).

It is doubtful that Italy was taken by Byzantium around 534 with the battle. The wife of the Byzantine emperor Justinian, named Theodora, is said to be the daughter of a bear keeper (dopteurs, circus). Like so many other stories, this one was probably invented by the time falsehoods in a somewhat adventurous manner. If such splendid buildings could be built in Ravenna, then after all not if you had previously wasted so much money on war, right? Because of the similarity of names, Theodora is more likely a daughter or niece of the Ostrogoth king Theodoric, whose mausoleum in Ravenna is also well known to tourists. According to the author, the Byzantine annexation of Italy could be more of an inheritance.

Byzantium immediately had its hands full holding Sicily against the Islamized Arabs.

However, the Arabs, for their part, are annoyed by the Vikings in Spain. In the period that followed, this Arab-Norman conflict expanded - as is known - to Sicily.

Just before the jump from 614 to 911 AD (within one year) are again (as in the period 500 to 550) now also in the period 550 to 600 AD clear facts created. The world in the Mediterranean area looks exactly the same around 600 as it did around 900. The time counterfeiters change it a little from 600 to 750, only to bring it back to the level of 600 from 750 to 900.

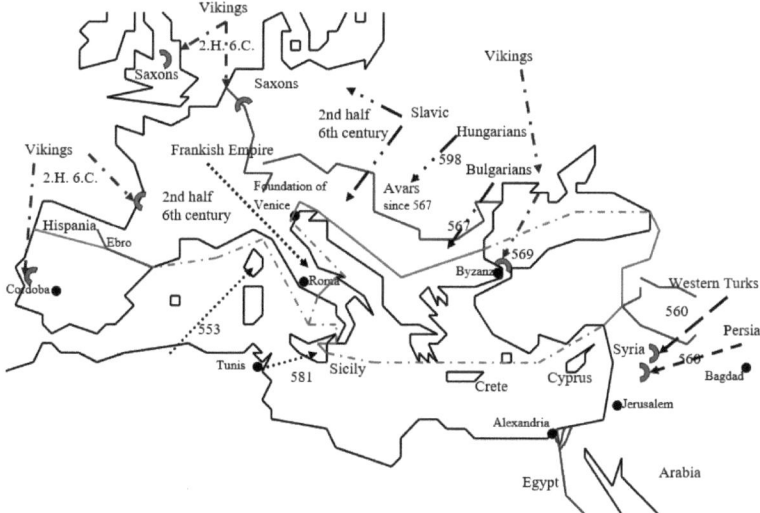

Pincer attack by the Vikings, Slavs westward: 550 to 600 AD

The military conditions in the 2nd half of the 6th century are as follows:

- 553 AD: Arabs conquer Corsica.
- around 560 AD: Persians, supported by the West Turks, continue to resist the Arab-Islamic tutelage and attack Syria again.
- 2nd half of the 6th century: Vikings attack the coasts of Western Europe again. Some of them settle in Britain and northern France. At the same time, the Vikings migrate south across Russian and Ukrainian rivers in order to reach Byzantium.
- 567 AD: Parts of the Avars (= Hungarians), Slavs and Bulgarians are pushed westward from their Russian settlement areas by the penetration of the Vikings, to the Elbe, into the Hungarian lowlands and into today's Bulgaria. (The irony of history: first Celtic and then Germanic areas now become Slavic through peaceful

evasion of the Slavs from the Vikings, who are related to the Germanic and Germanic peoples.)

- 569 AD: Vikings stand with their boats in front of Byzantium and besiege the city for a short time. The Western Turks are not only allies of the Persians, but also of the Byzantines. The Turks help defend Byzantium against the Vikings. (Another irony of history: Turkmens are getting an appetite for the Bosporus. From Antioch to Lübeck, peoples settle down that ancient man would never have suspected. The landscapes get completely new mentalities. At the same time, Germans and Arabs roam former areas of the Roman Empire.)
- until 581 AD: Arabs have almost all of Sicily in their hands. Only the city of Taormina can survive into the 7th = 10th century.

Aside from world events, (Lower) Saxony and (Rhine) Franconia in East Hesse are "getting into each other's wool". In the middle of the 6th century combat troops clash and there are numerous battles between the two Germanic tribes, including in Hesse and Thuringia. The Fulda Abbey, which was still in its infancy at the time, is also affected. The world only learns of this idyllic, remote corner of Europe through the suspected blood relationship between the historian Bishop Gregor von Tours and the first abbots of the Fulda monastery. Attalus, the grandson of Bishop Gregorius Attalus von Langres (living in Dijon), later Hatto Bonosus, built around 550 AD in Fulda a villa rustica, very anachronistic, but committed to tradition.

This villa may be destroyed by the Saxons in AD 556. Exactly 297 years later on September 1st, 853 AD the church property is stolen in the fictitious time. A hidden reference from a contemporary to the phantom time 614 to 911?

In Fulda even Arab envoys are received around 650 = around 950, which proves the luster faience found there. Abbot

Hademar (derived perhaps even from the Roman city Andematunum, is now called Langres near Dijon, and not from Germanic "famous through battle") travels to Rome several times, as does his nephew Hatto (derived from Attalus?) To order for Otto I. Saxony negotiate the imperial coronation with the Pope. You don't have to descend from an emperor yourself, such as from Attalus Priscus, counter-emperor around 410 and 414 AD, appointed by the Visigoths against Emperor Honorius, forced by the Visigoths to Christianity from the ancient belief in many gods and possibly the grandfather of an Attalus, leading Official in Autun. After all, Otto the Great's third wife, Adelheid, was also from Burgundy.

If 297 years can be left out, a genealogist may wonder if he could not find his ancestors in ancient times with this help. With the rulers, whether a Germanic king, a Byzantine emperor or a Roman pope, we know that the clans mostly die out violently again and again. The Merovingians start at 400 and don't go back any further. All famous family names of antiquity are as if extinguished from 550 and especially from 911. A Hademar is even sold as one of the sons of Charlemagne, so a respected name after all. Hatto could be derived from Attalus (Greek Attalos). Roman citizenship was granted around 560 and 580 AD dissolved. The obligation to use non-ancient family names went hand in hand with this. It is unclear with how much violence and murder this was enforced. The family of Gregory of Tours seems to be the only one who has a chance to venture a family tree from antiquity into the Middle Ages. Even with the beginning of the reign of the first soldier emperor Maximius Thrax in the first half of the 3rd century AD, we still have trouble finding classic republican Roman names among the consuls.

In addition, the (Rhine) Francs fall not only in (Lower) Saxony, but around 550 AD also entered Italy and, with the exception of southern Italy, wrested the territories from the

Byzantines. Ravenna, surrounded by swamps, is no longer sufficient on its own for the Italian population to be able to seek protection. Because the Franks invade Italy from the northwest and the Slavs from the northeast, the Italians founded Venice in a lagoon. A lot of trees from the Alps have to be brought in for the hardened stakes in the water to support the beautiful buildings, towers, bridges and squares.

It is also interesting that after the conquest of northern and central Italy in the second half of the 6th century, the Franks succeeded in abolishing Roman citizenship. The designation "comes" (citizen) is only permitted from the title of the count upwards. The population that does not manage to get hold of a secular or spiritual top title is mostly and in many areas without rights and serfs, whatever that may mean in practice in the early Middle Ages in contrast to late antiquity.

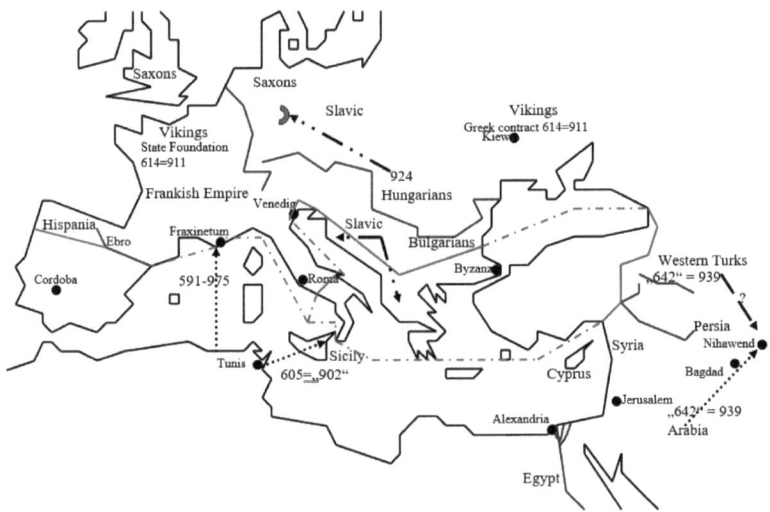

600 to 614 and 911 to 940: Same year 614 = 911 AD

The Arabs are still active in the western Mediterranean. Historically speaking, these are the last two wins of Islam, and there are just two cities, but the conquests in the West are still annoying one last time for Christianity and the old world: On the one hand, the last Christian base falls on Sicily, Taormina in the year 605 AD, on the other hand near Marseille in southern France with the city Fraxinetum (near Frejus) a bridgehead can be taken by Moorish pirates in the year 591. It was not until 940 (approx. 50 years later) that the Caliphate of Cordoba was found to have a great influence.

It is the decade of greatest need for Christianity in the West. The Arabs raid cities like Arles and Nice.
Looting trains from Fraxinetum to the south of Lyon and to Lake Geneva are reported. An advance by the Arabs to St. Gallen is probably invented, especially since the St. Gallen monastery is known for the strange building and garden plan in the middle of the phantom time and it is precisely at this time that it stands out.

In this emergency, Byzantium is asked for help. It was not until 975 that the Lower Saxon Ottonians, the Burgundians and Provençals as well as a Byzantine naval blockade were able to remove the Arab bridgehead. It had existed for almost 100 years: 975 minus 591 minus 297 equals 87 years!
Toulouse is also said to have been invaded again and again across the Pyrenees by the Arabs from Spain.

What is interesting now is exactly the year 614 = 911 AD This year marks the founding of the Viking states in Normandy in northern France as well as in the Ukraine around Kiev.

In order to pull the Vikings to the side of Christianity, a leap of 297 years is dared at this point, in which Islam is postponed from antiquity and Christianity can be portrayed in the proudest colors up to the fictional year 622. The undertaking succeeds. The Vikings take the side of the

Christians (despite Islamic proselytizing attempts) and receive two state treaties in the year 614 = 911, one for Normandy and one for the Kiev Empire.

The fact that the Byzantines let the time jump to 911 in 614 of all times, when the Vikings received two state treaties based on the Roman model, suggests that they told the Vikings a completely different story between 337 and 614/911 than actually took place. As already written, just so as not to run the risk of losing the Northmen to Islam.
The film "The 13th Warrior" certainly suggests the possibility of Islamic proselytizing attempts north of the Alps. After all, it is known that not only the Europeans, but also the Arabs and Chinese and other peoples have come far out into the world to spread their culture. So Islam came to Indonesia and far south from sub-Saharan Africa.

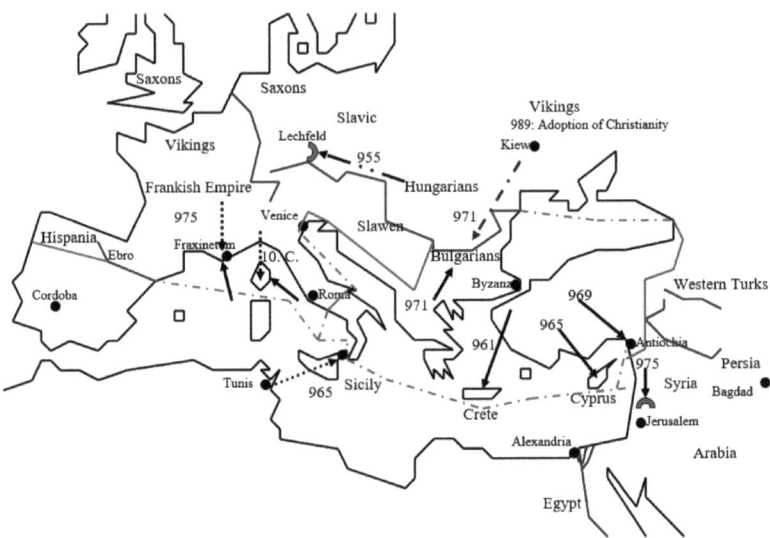

Stabilization of Europe through counter-attacks from 950 to 1000 AD

The first reconquest of "ancient Europe" under the leadership of Byzantium began in the 2nd half of the 10th century. There was plenty of time for that. 950 minus 337 minus 297 years equals 316 years. The islands of Corsica, Crete and Cyprus can be captured. However, Sicily still loses in 965 AD the very last base Rometta (near Messina) to the Arabs.

While the Vikings and Normans have come to rest a little with their state founding (in the 11th century they will conquer Sicily from the Arabs and southern Italy from the Byzantines), the Hungarians on the Lechfeld near Augsburg in 955 AD pacified by the (Lower) Saxons and pushed back into the Hungarian lowlands.

Western Europe is saved for now.

Why 297 years

Why are 297 years in use right now? The number is made up of the product 3x3x3x11. According to chronological critics, 33 is a magical number because this could have been the age of Jesus Christ, when he died on the cross on Golgotha.

However, this time interval also has a very practical benefit: It is not just that you have to pay attention to the "same" season when you jump from about 300 years, you have to go from mid-January to mid-January or the end of September to the end September must jump.

In addition, attention can also be paid to the day of the week. Maybe that's more important.
In 1582, too, the course of the weekdays was left untouched when jumping from October 4th to October 15th.

If now, on August 31, 614, the next day September 1, 911 follows, the computers of the world with their arithmetic programs will output that August 31, 614 was a Saturday and September 1, 911 was a Sunday.
So it was even the weekend and you can comfortably take a leap in time.

But this also means that on the fictitious August 31st 911 (actually 614) was also a Saturday and on the fictitious September 1st 614 (actually 911) it was also a Sunday, otherwise this consideration does not work.
But that's what it looks like ... because the computer program has been set up as if the 297 years in between actually existed. So that's exactly 297 years!
The transition from August 31, 614 to September 9, 911 is interesting for several reasons and it is a pity if Dr. Illig has not yet gone into this.

a) A Saturday on August 31, 614 is followed by a Sunday on September 9, 911
b) It takes place at that time in the middle of the year (more on that later)
c) Moving the Arabic time axis by 297 years into the past gives militarily traceable results, e.g. in the year 401 AD before Carthage (698, capture by Arabs) and northern Italy (401, invasion of the Visigoths). Not only then did we come across the appropriate difference of 297 years time and again.

The story is no more complicated than necessary.
One also appeals a little to the laziness of humans, the inner weaker self. The Romans and their pragmatic thinking left no room for overly complicated circuits in their Julian calendar.
According to the defenders of Charlemagne, how should the leap years from 46 BC to 1000 AD have run continuously if they mean 297 years between August 31st. 614 and Sept. 1, 911 in between?
Second, we also show here that with and without 297 years, Saturday is actually followed by a Sunday. Because here you can see that 300 years would not have been possible, because then another day of the week would have followed a Saturday.

But that's only one side. 297 fictitiously added years let the days of the week run through continuously, but then it jumps with the even switching of the leap years from 46 BC to 1000 AD. We know that every 100 years are divisible by four and that every full century in Julian Calendar is a leap year. The year 1600 and the year 2000 are also leap years. In the Gregorian calendar, the leap years 1700, 1800 and 1900, 2100 etc. are omitted. So 1600 was a leap year. Then 1500, 1400, 1300, 1200, 1100 and 1000 were also leap years.

With the Julian calendar there is (normally the regular leap years every 4 years factored in) every 28 years the same day of the week with respect to a certain date in the year. A May 16 on a Tuesday also falls on a Tuesday again after 28 years.

Now I'll go through the two cases:

a) There are no 297 years between 614 and 911:

So then I have 1000 minus 28 minus 28 minus 28 in the year 916 a leap year and also in the year 912 (shortly before the jump of 297 years). Because 614 is identical to 911, the previous leap year comes in 611. 912 yes, 911 not, 613 not, 612 not, but 611 yes.
It is astonishingly interesting how smoothly the time goes back to 46 BC, the first leap year:

Since 611 is a leap year, it is logically also 607 and 603 AD. You can see quite clearly here that people did not think in those years back then. It is only a subsequent adjustment to the new era. 46 BC nobody in Rome thought he was now living "46 BC". Everyone saw clairvoyantly and knew that in 46 years a child would be born in Judea, including Julius Caesar, "By Jupiter!"

If there is a leap year every 100 years, then before 603 AD there is also a leap year in the year 3 AD. Before that is the next 2 before Christ. Because the year zero does not exist. The year 1 BC is followed by the year 1 AD.
3 after Chr. Yes, 2 after Chr. No, 1 after Chr. No, 1 before Chr. No, 2 before Chr. Yes.
If 2 BC was a leap year, then 6, 10, 14, 18, 22, 26, 30, 34, 38, 42, and 46 BC are also leap years.
The Julian calendar was introduced in 46 BC.

b) The 297 years between 614 and 911 AD exist:

Then in AD 100 I the leap year and then 100 years earlier in the year 1 BC Then I miss the year 2 BC and thus the year 46 BC by 1 year and the switching of the leap years does not run continuously from 46 BC to 912 Chr.

One tries to explain this with the fact that 1 year does not count with more than 1000 years of history. Or that 46 BC should have had 365 plus 80 days, or that between 8 BC and 8 AD the correction was canceled because of the switching of every 3 years leap year from 46 BC to 8 BC.
Whoever has power on the globe always has an argument. And the poor like to look up to power.

Regarding the days of the week, as I said, it is not a problem whether we believe in Charlemagne or not. He looks like Santa Claus.
This figure does not exist. It could also be a fairy tale by the Brothers Grimm. Is the size of Otto the Great not enough for the Germans? Anyone who does not suspect the lie cannot be helped. Karl is canonized, although he slaughters the (Lower) Saxons. As brutally illogical as the Huns and Vandals.

If on September 9th, 912 is a Tuesday, then on the same day in 911 there was a Sunday because there was a February 29th, 912.

Minus 280 years and again minus 28 years results in the year 604 AD. There, September 1st, 604 is also a Tuesday. 608 it's a Sunday. 614 it is also a Sunday again. The 31.8.614 is a Saturday. You just have to draw the years between 604 and 614 individually.

The leap day falls on the same weekday every 28 years. E.g. it looks like this: 912 AD plus 28 equals 940 AD:

1.9.912 a Tuesday because leap year,
1.9.913 a Wed,
1.9.914 a Thu,
1.9.915 a Fri,
1.9.916 a Sunday, because leap year,
1.9.917 a Mon,
1.9.918 a Tue,
1.9.919 a Wed,
1.9.920 a Fri, because leap year,
1.9.921 a Sat,
1.9.922 a Sun,
1.9.923 a Mon,
1.9.924 a Wed, because leap year,
1.9.925 a Thu,
1.9.926 a Fri,
1.9.927 a Sat,
1.9.928 a Mon, because leap year,
1.9.929 a Tue,
1.9.930 a Wed,
1.9.931 a Thu,
1.9.932 a Sat, because leap year,
1.9.933 a Sun,
1.9.934 a Mon,
1.9.935 a Tue,
1.9.936 a Thu, because leap year,
1.9.937 a Fri,
1.9.938 a Sat,
1.9.939 a Sun,
1.9.940 a Tuesday because leap year.

After 28 years, the leap day February 29 is again on the same weekday.

912 minus 280 results in the fictitious year 632.
632 minus 28 results in 604.
In all these years, September 1st is a Tuesday.

Then
1.9.608 a Sun,
1.9.612 a Fri,
1.9.613 a Sat,
1.9.911 a Sun.

Blurring traces, e.g. beginning of the year

A whole series of measures have been taken by the time falsifiers around the year 1000 AD to "blur" the insertion of 297 fictitious years between 614 and 911 AD:

First, it probably lends itself to depicting what the calendar once looked like:

In today's official historiography it is claimed that the shifting of the beginning of the year from March 1 to January 1 happened before Caesar's birth, in 153 BC. The consuls would have enforced this at that time together with the city of Rome, for which reason? Thus the time falsifiers maintain it and impute this to the Roman consuls.

It seems to me rather in such a way that only in the course of this time falsification around 600 to 1000 AD the 1st January was explained to the beginning of the year, in order to cover traces of the time falsification.

Some other things have been done around 600 AD.

The year "46 before Chr." should have been all at once oversized long, namely instead of 365 days, it would have had 445 days, thus exactly 80 days longer.
Allegedly one attached the days to February and to November. Of it the Otto normal consumer has never heard what, also not in the best history instruction in the school.

Apart from the fact that in the history books an extension of this year 46 is not necessarily noticeable, these 80 days nevertheless uncover something. One must count the days only intelligently starting from 1 January.

80 = 31 days of January + 28 days of February + 21 days of March.

Instead of adding the days in November and February, one can also go through the time from January 1 to March 21 twice to get the year 46 before Christ to a length of 445 days. Whether the year begins now with 1. March or 1. January plays a subordinate role here. The decisive fact is that the forgers have probably fooled themselves again. Because it can mean only that the beginning of spring in the year 46 before Christ has lain on the 21st March.

According to the author, the beginning of the year was shifted from March 1 to January 1 only around 1000 AD and the year 46 BC had the usual 365 days and not 445 days.

A confusing statement of the officials is already, if
a) At the Council of Nicaea the 21st March was the beginning of spring.
b) 46 before Chr. also on 21. March spring beginning is (or another part says, one does not know it suddenly any more).
c) 46 before Chr. to 10 before Chr. every 3 years a 29th February was switched.
d) 10 before Chr. a correction should have been executed until 8 AD on order of emperor Augustus.
e) This order had not been executed however.

46 minus 10 equals 36 years. Divided by 4 are 9, divided by 3 are 12. That means 3 switching days are switched too much. Then suddenly the 21st March is no longer the beginning of spring, but (within 36 years) the 18th March. If that would be so, then between 10 before and 325 AD 5 or 6 times the leap year would have had to fail, in order to let it come out 325 with 21 March.
What now. That runs nevertheless even into the wrong direction.

Besides this does not go so, if the people around 46 before Chr. the spring beginning on 21. March knew, then afterwards something else can have happened. It does not go that 21. March 325 AD is again beginning of spring, if one assumes that the leap years run through all 4 years from 46 to 325 normally. If not, then either 46 BC is wrong or 325 AD is wrong. Neither works unless there was a jerky movement of the earth. This is how chronology critic Immanuel Velikovsky tries to explain the alleged error in the Julian calendar. But it is not known that something changed the orbital period of the earth around the sun. Here a celestial body of about the same weight would have had to come close enough to the earth. Of it nothing is known. So it probably does not go still more complicated!?

One year after the omission of the 10 days 1583 was in any case 21. March in the Vatican the beginning of spring.

Another topic as already written: In the school one gets well-behaved taught, in Caesar's times the beginning of spring was on the 21st March. Hardly asks then times a chronology critic like Dr. Illig more exactly, then it is suddenly in such a way that to the council of Nikia 325 AD the beginning of spring falls on 21 March and thus to Caesar time on 24 March. It is suddenly said that it is actually not at all provable when the beginning of spring was actually in Caesar's time. That says even Dr. Illig: Actually there is no 100% proof.

But probably there is also no 100% proof when the beginning of spring was in 325 AD.

The author would like to question at this point the 21. March once fundamentally. Why is such an arbitrary day in the month the beginning of spring at all. It is not a special day in the month in Rome!

March 1st: beginning of spring in 130 BC?

The thought of "March 1st" came to me in May 2004.
The basic question of the author is actually very simple.

Why one argues about the exact day of the beginning of spring on March 21 or March 24 and does not consider why it was not put sensibly on March 1, on the beginning of the year at that time!
March 21 is just as little a special day in the Roman calendar as March 24.

That now the 1st of March could have been beginning of spring, is now not at all handed down. Also inscriptions in stone do not point to it.
Nevertheless, the question arises whether Caesar was the first Roman who introduced the solar calendar in Rome. Or whether he only had the leap day "February 29" introduced exactly every four years, by his Egyptian scholar Sosigenes, in order to correct the grossest.

Several assumptions without any basis are necessary here. It concerns here so to speak a pure thought experiment:

The Romans took their first scientific calendar from the Greeks. The Greeks worked after the moon. Likewise the Persians proceeded in the antiquity. Only the Egyptians aligned their calendar after the sun.

The previous historiography possibly wrongly assumes that we still have a lunar calendar with the Romans until 46 BC and a solar calendar only from 46 BC on.

The lunar calendar was plausibly a firmly established size in the Roman state system up to the late republican phase. Therefore it cannot be assumed as finished too early before 46 BC to explain the 1st or 21st or 24th of March.

The question is now, which calendar manages to advance the beginning of spring from March 1 to March 21 or 24 within a few decades?

A very fast advance one accomplishes with a solar calendar with which leap years were renounced in principle! On all leap years!

We know from Egypt that there the priests prevented the introduction of leap years successfully also against the desire of the Pharaos Ptolemäus (Macedonian general under Alexander the Great).
Such a calendar could have been introduced also by the Romans. Then they could have determined that it becomes quite fast impractical, because sowing and harvests had to be taken up all 4 years in each case one day "later". Each year had 365 days and thus every 4 years was about one day short. Thus the yearly beginning March 1st took place seasonally seen ever earlier and moved ever more into the winter.

If we assume that March 21 is correct in the year 46 BC, when the first leap day February 29 became law for the first time in Roman history at the end of that year, then the simplest solar calendar - i.e. one without leap years - was introduced in 129 BC. This could refer to the legacy of Pergamum in 133 BC and the many Roman state reforms between 133 and 130 AD.

If in 46 BC the beginning of spring had fallen on March 24 (and thus not until the Council of Nicaea in 325 AD on March 21), then such a calendar should have started in 141 BC. One destroyed 146 before Chr. Carthago in Tunisia and Corinth in Greece.
One must prove now only that one would have taken over no calendar from Carthage, the mortal enemy, anyway, even if they could have had a solar calendar from Egypt. And one

must show that Pergamon could have had a solar calendar. Corinth in Greece probably kept the lunar calendar.

In purely mathematical terms:

$$(21 - 1) \, days \, / \, (365.00 - 365.2422) \, days/year \, = \, 82.6 \, years.$$

46 before Chr. + 82.6 results then in the year 129 BC.

Now the senators gathered since 133 before Chr. to many meetings, in order to accomplish a large reform in the state system because of the impoverishment of the farmers in Italy and because of the inheritance of Pergamon. In the process, because of the intransigence of the patricians, there was a revolt under Tiberius Gracchus, the representative of the common people. Tiberius was killed, and years later his brother was also killed.

If March 24 had been in effect in Caesar's time, a solar calendar would have been introduced 94.96 years earlier ... according to:

$$(24 - 1) \, days \, / \, (365.00 - 365.2422) \, days/year.$$

Which of the two parties is to be given now right because of the 21st of March? Council of Nicaea 325 after Chr. or Caesar 46 before Chr.?

The so-called Anno Domini notation is introduced by the way only at the end of the 15th century, when one just discovered the new world. Only from then on we can assume that the calendar of the Persians was synchronized with that of Europe for the first time. At the beginning of the Renaissance, however, the falsification of time was already very long ago.
However, centuries before the "year count after Christ's birth" was officially introduced, only in 600 AD it was also

600 years after Christ's birth and in 1000 AD it was only 700 years.

Because of the elliptical course of the earth around the sun one has already trouble to let fall further beginnings of the seasons likewise on a 21st (originally 1st). With the beginning of autumn one would have only a chance, if July and August had 32 days in each case and November for it 28 days. Of all things July and August carry the names of the two largest Roman rulers. In the middle somewhere in the year or at that time in the middle of the first half of the year. This cannot be a coincidence!

Each season beginning spring, summer, autumn and winter had the 1st of a month (around 130 before Chr.), then it had the 21st of a month (around 46 before Chr.), also the beginning of autumn. Then at the Council of Nicaea in 325 AD it was the 18th of a month.

Also, days were rearranged in the early Middle Ages to cover tracks, so that the beginning of autumn falls on a 23rd. Therefore, July and August probably had 32 days and November and February had 28 days. February was the last month of the year until around 1000 AD.

Perhaps the forgers pretend also therefore, to February and to November days 46 before Chr. were attached, because both months had 28 days.

Why the signs of the zodiac no longer fit into the original months, because slipped by 21 days, is now clear.

Aries formerly belonged completely in March, Gemini in May and Leo in July. If you remember the first week of August 2003 with its heat of 40 degrees in the shade, you know that July was once the hottest month and the zodiac sign Leo still reflects that today.

You can also see it in the weather. Not the today's beginning of the month makes a weather change, but rather the one week before the change of the month. While 46 before Chr.

everything had already slipped by 21 days, 129 before Chr. everything was still in the best order. Only the signs of the zodiac are today still at their seasonally correct position. This was not caused by the Byzantine government or the Christian church, but by the scientific ignorance of the Romans in the final phase of the Republic. Or the good faith towards the Egyptian or possibly the Pergamenian calendar.

Initial situation 129 +/- 1 before Chr:
- 1st March beginning of spring and beginning of the year,
- Introduction of solar calendar without leap years.

The signs of the zodiac were 129 before Chr. still exactly in their month as follows:

Aries = March (first month in the year), 31 days, spring.
Taurus = April (second month of the year), 30 days
Gemini = May (third month of the year), 31 days.
Cancer = June (fourth month of the year), 30 days, summer
Leo = July (fifth month of the year), 32 days.
Virgo = August (sixth month of the year), 32 days.
Libra = September (seventh month of the year), 30 days, autumn.
Scorpio = October (eighth month of the year), 31 days.
Sagittarius = November (ninth month of the year), 28 days
Capricorn = December (tenth month in the year), 31 days, winter
Aquarius = January (eleventh month of the year), 31 days
Pisces = February (twelfth month of the year), 28 days

So in 130 BC, October was the suicide month and not November as it was from 46 BC or 1582 AD, although Scorpios are perhaps the least suicidal.

Therefore, the beginning of spring in Caesar's time must fall on March 21, and: Between 46 BC and 1582 AD actually about 300 years less have passed than official history would have us believe.

If one lets now apply until 46 before Chr. a solar calendar without leap years, then the beginning of spring runs forward as follows from 1. March to 21. March. The speed of the progress per year is independent of it whether I accept the years 614 to 911 as genuine or not. Only the exact times vary. Because, if one lets calculate this with a common formula over the calculator, and the formula takes the year 1582 as a basis, then one must subtract 297 years. One pretends therefore, as if the progress of around 130 before Chr. to 46 before Chr. in the years of around 167 after Chr. to 251 after Chr. would have taken place.

Year before Chr. / Day of spring / hour / minute

131 BC / March 1/4 a.m. / 21.5 min
130 BC / March 1/10 a.m. / 11.2 min
129 BC / March 1/3 p.m. / 57.7 min
128 BC / March 1/9 p.m. / 49.3 min
127 BC / March 2/3 a.m. / 32.2 min
126 BC / March 2/9 a.m. / 25.5 min
125 BC / March 2/3 p.m. / 28.3 min
124 BC / March 2/9 p.m. / 14.7 min
123 BC / March 3/3 a.m. / 4.8 min
122 BC / March 3/8 a.m. / 59.2 min
etc.
58 BC / March 18/8 p.m. / 47.1 min
57 BC / March 19/2 a.m. / 40.5 min
56 BC / March 19/8 a.m. / 24.8 min
55 BC / March 19/2 p.m. / 10.2 min
54 BC / March 19/8 p.m. / 10.8 min
53 BC / March 20/2 a.m. / 1.6 min
52 BC / March 20/7 a.m. / 48.4 min
51 BC / March 20/1 p.m. / 40.3 min
50 BC / March 20/7 p.m. / 28.7 min
49 BC / March 21/1 a.m. / 25.2 min
48 BC / March 21/7 a.m. / 11.8 min
47 BC / March 21/12 noon / 52.7 min
46 BC / **March 20**/6 p.m. / 47.6 min
45 BC / March 21/12 midnight / 34.2 min
44 BC / March 21/6 a.m. / 16.5 min
43 BC / March 21/12 noon / 11.1 min
42 BC / **March 20**/5 p.m. / 59.6 min

130 - 46 BC	46 BC - 1582(-297)AD	since 1582(-297)AD
every year with 365 days?	every forth year with 366 days	but not every 400th year

I suggest that Caesar only introduced the leap year and that the solar calendar was introduced around 130 BC +/- 1.

Actual reason for lying in time

The situation became extremely critical for Christianity around 600 AD.
Islam had invaded numerous central European territories in the west from Spain and Tunisia at that time, including southern France and the west coast of Italy.
On the other hand, the Byzantines heard of efforts by the Arabs to proselytize the Russians and Vikings to Islam.
Both were not to be!

The Christianity stands in better light, if one discusses the Islam, shortly after toleration of the Christianity in the Roman empire in Milan, wrongly by 297 years into the future.

Because the reality means that already few years after Constantine's death the city Jerusalem is between 340 AD and 1097 (minus 297) AD thus for 460 years (up to the 1st crusade) in Islamic hand.

One must imagine that once:

297 years are inserted only because then Christianity has time at all to build itself up as a state religion. Jerusalem is - so we are led to believe - still 300 years in Christian hands.

At this point, it may be helpful to know that Islam borrows, among other things, from Christian and Jewish sects that existed in Palestine only until around 400 AD. Thus, according to Dr. Illig and other chronology critics, it is unlikely that Muhammad should have waited another 200 years before appearing on the stage of world history.

Huns, Vandals, Spanish Visigoths

Especially Huns and Vandals are strongly denigrated in today's history. One meets the two tribes with much disgust. Yet Huns did not even exist, neither those who invaded Europe, nor those who invaded Persia. And the Vandals have already been defeated on the Danube near Vienna or Budapest and never got as far as Spain let alone Tunisia. The Visigoths only reached the northern Spanish river Ebro because the Arabs met them there.

Even von Goethe (*Frankfurt, +Weimar) speaks of a strangely mysterious people when he mused about the Huns. A people that came out of the dark and disappeared again in the dark. Archaeologically, there is actually nothing. Much sounds like something out of a fairy tale. Plots are (murder of the Hun leader by a Germanic scalvine) somewhat immature and handed down like the Nibelungen saga. The origin is assumed to be in one of the most remote areas of the world: Afghanistan. Of all places, they are supposed to come from there, from a country where so many great powers have already failed. A people who live in a region where they have nothing to fear from the outside will not want to conquer half the world. Where is the impetus here?

If, however, only Avars, Hungarians and Slavs broke in from the East, then that is already more than enough. Why do Christian time falsifiers have to lie here and salt the soup of history. The Eastern peoples were pushed westward by the Ukrainian Vikings, in the 6th century.

The Huns represent only one explanatory reason why the Germanic peoples were driven so strongly into the Roman Empire in the course of their migration. They evaded the pressure of the Huns.

But if now the Arabs destroy the Roman empire from the south, and this already directly after 337 AD, then it is only logical, if the Teutons participate in the fall of Rome or want to secure the best places for themselves or were even called to help by the Romans and Greeks, although the latter is rather improbable.

If one puts the history of Islam 300 years earlier (as actually happened), then there is no need for Huns. Germanic tribes and Arabs divided the Roman Empire, with the exception of Byzantium, as booty.

The high tempo of the Arabs in North Africa thus becomes plausible: competition with the Teutons for the booty of Rome.

The interference in Persian throne disputes in the 5th century by the Huns is purely in Greek (forged) sources. The Persians themselves never wrote such a thing down. If the history of Islam begins 300 years earlier and consequently stops between 614 and 911, then the Arabs (and not the Huns) interfered in the affairs of government of the Persians. When the Arabs could conquer nothing new in the West, they set their sights on Persia. It was not until the end of the 10th century that this religion gained a foothold beyond the Zagros Mountains.

About the Vandals just as heavily one pulls down. Yet the "poor" did much less damage. That is almost typical, if over a fictitious, invented action (destruction of antique buildings from Spain to Tunisia) a term develops: Vandalism.

About a fact that did not happen, people like to make light of it. A rather dull desire that suits the medieval petty bourgeois.

As said, the Vandals were already devastated at the Danube near Budapest by the Romans and their Germanic allies and did not reach Italy, Spain or even Tunisia. The attack from Tunisia by sea on the city of Rome in the 5th century is certainly due to the Arabs.

While Huns are completely from the imagination, Vandals have existed, but were prematurely beaten out of history, already around 400 AD.

The Visigoths, for their part, only got as far as the Ebro River near Barcelona. For there the Arabs and Visigoths clashed.

From Egypt via Pergamon to Rome

It is not known how the solar calendar could have come from Egypt to Pergamum, possibly to be inherited from there to Rome in 133 BC.

It is not known today to which calendar the kings of Pergamon kept. It is only known that a certain Attalos, probably identical with King Attalos III, had letter contact with the best astronomer of ancient times, Hipparchus of Nicaea (city southeast of Istanbul, council of 325 AD). Hipparch was born around 190 BC in Nicaea and died around 120 BC probably in Rhodes.

Hipparchus was the first surviving astronomer in human history to mathematically measure the heavens and calculate distances. He created a new star catalog and compared it with older catalogs. Amazingly exact for that time he determined the distance between earth and moon to 33.67 earth diameter and the moon diameter to 0.33 earth diameter. To estimate the distance to the sun with 1245 earth diameter was however too little. With an earth diameter of 12742 km this is 429023 km to the moon according to Hipparch. In reality it is 384400 km on average (because of the elliptic orbit the orbit varies between 363300 and 405500 km).

The distance to the sun would be 12742 x 1245 = 15863790 km. This is about 10 times too little. In addition he calculated the wobbling of the earth, which rotates like a gyroscope, so that in 14000 years the old position is reached again, and the today's polar star did not have this function in Roman times. Within the 14000 years cycle the bright shining star Vega is also times north star.
The year length was fixed relatively exactly by Hipparchus to 365 days, 5 hours, 55 minutes and 12 seconds.

This friend Attalos could have been also the last king of Pergamon, although this is not written so in the Pauly-Wissowa, the standard work for the description of antique persons. King Attalos III cared little for the affairs of state and was strongly focused on natural science (many individual disciplines). He may have died in an experiment. It may be that the king had included the solar calendar as a recommendation in his inheritance to the Romans, with strong support from Hipparchus of Nicaea, who had done research in Rhodes and Egypt.

Pergamon had the largest library of the ancient world after Egypt in the 2nd century BC. And after the Egyptians refused to supply papyrus to Pergamum, the Pergamenians simply invented parchment.
It was an extremely tolerant city, where people celebrated vigorously.

The initially dwarf state of Pergamon came into being because Philetairos, a colonel of General Lysimachus, comrade-in-arms of Alexander the Great and lion conqueror, had to guard a state treasure at Pergamon Castle. When Lysimachus fell in battle against Seleucus, the Macedonian Philetairos, unmolested, used the huge treasure for his own purposes and founded a tiny kingdom among all the vast empires, successor states of Alexander the Great.

The famous temple of the city of Pergamon was rebuilt in Berlin. According to some Christians, it is the temple of the devil. But "please gentlemen", what is this impudence to insult such nice rulers!?
Sometimes I wonder who are the heathens here.

One repetition to deepen

One cannot avoid, if one takes out periods, to question numerous rulers. Charlemagne and with him his complete family are pure invention. This was stated or suggested by Dr. Illig. Also all popes and emperors in Byzantium have sprung from the imagination between 614 and 911.

But what about the Arab and Persian side?

If I agree with Mr. Illig, then this has even more serious implications than what he had described in his books so far. It is true that he has the courage to deny the Carolingian family completely, which the author would not have dared to do. But then it would suit him to follow up on Islam and the Arab invasion of the Roman Empire.

The Islamic conquests of the Arabs from 634 AD (actually from 337 AD) are realistic, if one first considers only Syria, Egypt to Spain. That with Persia did not run completely so simply and differently, as today represented. Here, however, in principle the time between 614 and 911 also does not exist.

If therefore these military events of the Arabs took place in such a way in the temporal order and also with their time quantity, then they must be pushed inevitably into the Christian time 317 to 614, because the period from 614 to 911 is fictitious with the Christians.

In other words, one could also state:
South of the Mediterranean the time from 317 to 614 is fictitious and north of the Mediterranean the time from 614 to 911.

If, however, one falsely retains the time between 614 to 911, then one can only make the following statement:

While in the northern Mediterranean region the migration of the Germanic tribes brings down the Roman Empire, in the south almost nothing happens. It was not until 300 years later that the Islamized Arabs overran the Roman Empire there. How does that fit together? Sounds a bit illogical, especially since one may assume that the Teutons would never have managed the collapse on their own. Their strength is not sufficient for that. A joint raid would make the collapse of the Roman Empire seem absolutely logical. The Arabs (with Persian help) have begun the fall of the Roman empire from 337 AD even before the Teutons!

Dr. Illig also points out: The teachings of Islam are very similar to a sect in Palestine, which existed only until about 400 AD. The merchant Mohammed from Mecca would have been born then probably approx. 270 AD and would have taken over the teachings very closely.

Why did Arabia bother to found its own religion?
It must have been because there was a danger that within free Arabia Christians would spy for Rome, seize control, and then incorporate even free Arabia down to Yemen into the Roman Empire. Therefore, the Arabs (including those in Palestine, if possible) must remain free from the Christian faith of the Romans. The unfree Arabs in Palestine can be won as allies in case of emergency, if one invades the Roman Empire. And so it came to pass.

The massive power vacuum immediately after Constantine's death was used without hesitation to invade the Roman Empire in 337.

An extremely striking point is the year 401.
It is logically understandable when, at the same time, the Visigoths invade northern Italy and the Arabs finally conquer the city of Carthage, which has been under siege for

decades. For troops of the Romans have to be withdrawn to Italy to protect the city of Rome.

It only takes another 9 years until Rome's center is sacked by the Visigoths in 410. The Teuton Stilicho merely stops the "barbarians" on behalf of the Romans at Verona in 402 and at Pollenca in 403. The Arabs, meanwhile, had already moved as far as Spain in 410 plus 297 equals 707 and crossed the Strait of Gibraltar in 414.

The Arab rulers between 614 and 911 belong to the time from 317 to 614. Here there is no problem, because on the Arabian peninsula officially between 317 and 614 almost no history is written, also not by the Christians. But there is a reference to a Christian invasion from Ethiopia around 300 AD on Arabia, to keep the story exciting. This can have taken place. But not necessarily the 2nd from Christian Ethiopia on Arabia in the 6th century.

With the Persians, the rulers seem to be relatively credible until about 600 AD. Certainly they are under pressure from Islam and the Arabs from about 450 AD, when the Arab onslaught on the Roman Empire largely comes to a halt. The invented Huns are also a substitute for Persia for the actual influence of the Arabs from the 5th century in Persia. The Persian great kings in those centuries are almost all members of the Sassanid house.

The northern Iranian tribe of Bujids based around Tehran seems to convert all Persia to Islam with military power in the 10th century. Therefore, Tehran becomes the modern capital of Persia. It is no longer Kteisophon, no longer Persepolis or any other city. The move of the Arabs has been invented and simply rewritten into the non-existent 7th century. It is significant here that the first All-Iranian ruler from the tribe of the Bujids calls himself "King of Kings", just as the Sassanids did last in the 6th century. If one leaves out the time between 614 and 911 in Persia, then there are not centuries between Bujids and Sassanids, but only decades.

In contrast to the Arabs on the Arabian peninsula and the Arabs who settled in Mesopotamia (Iraq) in the course of time, the Bujids are not Sunnis but Shiites. Through them, a separate form of Islam emerges in Persia and southern Iraq. Thus, the Persians or a tribe of Persians has it in their hands to create their own form. This speaks for a certain independence from the Arabs.

The Arab rulers in Persia between 614 and 911 described by Christian chroniclers (from Mesopotamia, from Armenia and from Bzyanz) are partly invented or have probably ruled as substitutes for the Huns parallel to the time of the Sassanids as "sub-kings". Roughly estimated half of the time, i.e. 150 years has sprung from the imagination like a fairy tale from 1001 nights and the other half of 150 years has been falsified in the rank of their rule too far into the future by the chroniclers. However, this should be investigated further.

Corrected Roman to Arabic-Islamic calendar

There are many people who do not understand the transition from late antiquity to the early Middle Ages in many parts of the world, precisely because this was where cheats were made and 614 to 911 was invented.

Other people who vehemently defend Charlemagne claim that if Charlemagne does not exist then Caesar, Napoleon and Hitler could just as well be fictional.

But I can't agree with that. The latter three show the global impact. Not with Charlemagne. Here the empire is as big at the beginning of its reign as it is at its end. The Carolingian era looks like an opera from the Swabian and Alemannic Staufer times.

These 300 European years from 614 to 911 are meaningless in relation to the interaction between different nations. While the story mostly takes place clearly above water, in the Carolingian era one feels like a drowned man who is laboriously allowed to gasp for air, who cannot understand anything that is going on around him in the fresh air, because something is deceiving him.

In the following, the timelines of the various peoples and empires are given, assuming the missing time between 614 and 911 AD matched. It's not that easy because you can't start with 614.

If one shifts the Arab events from 614 to 911 to the years 317 to 614, then one would be forced to consider what could have happened on the Arabian Peninsula between 317 and 614.

With the Persians this is not necessary because the events there between 300 and 600 essentially (e.g. ruler's names) remain untouched. Only the understanding of the role of Romans and Arabs is given a different weighting. However, the time in Persia between approx. 600 and approx. 900 is just as invented as it is forged in Italy, Gaul, Germania, Britain, etc. So one has only blinded the Arabs by postponing their Islam and the history of the Arab conquest by 300 years.

The Christian chroniclers understood that nowadays one has to consider how the Arab rulers IN Persia between 614 and 911 can be explained. Not really, because it doesn't exist. Between 337 and 950 Persia came to terms with Islam, only from 950 AD did it adopt it. Because the time between 614 and 911 does not exist, there are only about 330 years between 325 and 950 AD.

That means we generally have a 300 year rhythm:

- Christianity arises in Augustus and Tiberius times
- During the time of Constantine, Islam was born in Arabia
- from 932 AD Islam is adopted in Persia

Because of the lack of historically significant contacts between the Vikings and the Romans and Greeks before 614 AD you are hardly forced to deal with 300 to 600 here as well. Everything that apparently happened to the Vikings between 793 and 911 actually happened between 496 and 911 (there are barely 120 years between them!). People pretended to hear about the Vikings in Rome for the first time in the fictional year 793. In fact, it was the year 496.

The fights and deals on the (Saudi) Arabian peninsula between the Arab tribes and against or with Rome 1 to 300 AD basically run similar to the contacts between Rome and Persia. All in all, it all looks very logical and is steeped in ancient mentality and humor.

The time from 300 AD is now unclear. in Arabia.

According to the timetable by Eberhard Serauky in his book "Im Glanze Allahs" we have the following events on the Arabian Peninsula:

- 26 BC Roman military advances as far as southern Arabia
- 106 AD the Sinai Peninsula becomes the Roman province of "Arabia"
- 300 AD Christian Ethiopia invades southern Arabia
- 525 AD Ethiopia occupies southern Arabia [297 years earlier]
- 570 AD Birth of Muhammad [297 years earlier]
- 570 AD Sassanids occupy Yemen (in southern Arabia) [unrealistic around 570, more likely around 270 AD]

It looks as if the Christian chroniclers are inventing Christian (!) Ethiopia against Arabia, just like the Huns against the Persians and against Rome, in order to divert attention from the invented 297 years or to fictitiously fill the gap with action.

At least the second attack by the Ethiopians on southern Arabia seems to be an invention to fill the time south of the Mediterranean and south of the Euphrates, invented between 317 and 614, with life.

But the Arabs have had since 337 AD started with Islam to conquer North Africa and Spain (until 417 AD). Subsequently, it is not the Huns (as Christian chroniclers want us to know), but the Arabs that pose a threat to the Persians.

There is enough space in Arab history to compress events on the peninsula from 600 years to 300 years. Arab history has been corrected for the actual events and set back exactly 297 years to the actual point in time. So nothing for Charlemagne fans. Long live the ancient world. It will hurt some who attribute their legitimacy to Charlemagne. Because these people still have power and influence today, Charlemagne continues to be sold as real.

But now to the parallel running events:

- * means: corrected by 297 years back to the correct event

- ** means phantom year (sometime between 615 and 910)
- *** means corrected by 297 years to the correct time in the future

---

313 after Christ:
Event north of the Mediterranean (Romans, Teutons): 313 Milan Edict of Tolerance; Emperors Constantine and Licinius tolerate Christianity
Event south of the Mediterranean (Arabs): 313 * Prophet Mohammed Revelation of God with the help of the Archangel Gabriel

---

325 after Christ:
Event north of the Mediterranean (Romans, Teutons): 325 Council of Nicaea

Event south of the Mediterranean (Arabs): 325 * Mohammed flees his hometown Mecca because of violent arguments

---

337 after Christ:
Event north of the Mediterranean (Romans, Teutons): 337 Death of Constantine the Great. He is succeeded by his three weak sons in the capitals of Rome, Byzantium and York.

Event south of the Mediterranean (Arabs): 337 * Battle of Ajnadein (city south of Jerusalem, between the Roman Empire and Persia). For the first time - after long internal struggles for Islam and supremacy over all of Arabia - the Arabs invade the Roman Empire.

---

338 after Christ:
Event north of the Mediterranean (Romans, Teutons): 338 see under "Arabs" and under "Mesopotamia and Persia"

Event south of the Mediterranean (Arabs):
338 * Roman Damascus (Syria) conquered by the Islamized Arabs. Sections of the city population sided with the Arabs and opened the gates to them.

Event in Mesopotamia and Persia:
338 The then Roman Nisibis (today on the Syrian-Turkish border) is besieged for the first time by the Persians (also 346 and 350, finally handed over to the Persians in 363)

---

339 to 341 after Christ:

Event north of the Mediterranean (Romans, Teutons):
340 Constantius II, Emperor of the Eastern Empire (Byzantium), wages war against the Persians [officially from 340]; [unofficially at the same time from 637 **] probably also against the Arabs.
340 Death of Constantius 'brother Constantine II (Britain) in Italy when the third brother Constans tried to conquer Italy [therefore no help for Constantius II against Arabs and Persians!].
341 Battle of Constans (Kaiser Westroms) against the Franks. [The remaining brother of Constantius has his hands full against a Germanic tribe, which at that time settled on the Lower Rhine and pressed on the borders of the Roman Empire. The Arab-Persian attack has meanwhile "got around" among the Germans.]
341 to 348 The Goths join Arian Christianity; Bible translation into Gothic by Bishop Ulfila. [In contrast to Rome, Byzantium can keep the Germanic tribe of Goths, who then settled on the lower Danube, peaceful and even evangelize them to Christianity.]

Event south of the Mediterranean (Arabs):
339 * to 341 * two-year siege of Jerusalem, only four years after Constantine's death the city is taken. [Disaster for Christianity!]

339 * Alleged Arab invasion of Iraq (Mesopotamia). [The attack front is extremely stretched by Egypt, Palestine, Syria AND Iraq. Because the Arabs also need the Persians, who also rule Iraq, as allies against Rome, this attack on Iraq is clearly fictitious. An attack in 933 would be possible instead of 636 **]

Event in Mesopotamia and Persia:
339 * to 341 * Persians probably take part in the siege of Jerusalem as an ally of the Arabs. The sole possession of Jerusalem in the years 614 ** to 628 ** is absolutely fictional. The exaggerated number of Christian victims alone could point to this (see also the execution of the Cologne virgins in the phantom time, where the number of victims is extremely unbelievable as well as the event itself does not fit into this time.).

----

342 to 344 after Christ:

Event north of the Mediterranean (Romans, Teutons):
342 Peace between Constans (Emperor of the Western Empire) and the Franks. [The Romans in the West have noticed that they have to come to an agreement with the Franks relatively quickly. There is too much at stake for that.]

Event south of the Mediterranean (Arabs):
343 * Battle of Heliopolis, i.e. Islam wins Egyptian soil for the first time. In addition to the Greek foundation by the Ptolemies, the Islamic city of Cairo is being rebuilt.
344 * All of Egypt (with the exception of Alexandria) in the hands of the Arabs.

Event in Mesopotamia and Persia:
344 Victory of the Byzantines (Constantius II) against the Persians at Singara (Sinjar) (south of Nisibis) [unofficially, possibly also defensive battle against the Arabs, because

Islam is close to today's Turkey; however, the Arabs are more concerned with conquering Egypt and stabilizing their rule in Syria and Palestine.]

344 * Persian Mosul conquered by Arabs [according to the official chronology; That sounds implausible, however, because the Persians were allies of the Arabs at the time; Alternative: Author postpones 641 ** to 938 ***, then: Coalition of Arabs, Western Turks and Iranian Bujids could have conquered Mosul. Christian chroniclers have a free hand here to falsify time.]

----

345 to 348 after Christ:

Event north of the Mediterranean (Romans, Teutons):
see under "Arabs" and "Mesopotamia and Persia"

Event south of the Mediterranean (Arabs):
345 * Islam moves into Alexandria (Egypt), the last bastion of the Romans or Byzantines in Egypt thus finally falls before 350 AD (!).
345 * Islam shortly before Libya. The way to the west in North Africa is now unhindered to the Arabs (with Persian auxiliaries) up to Carthage.
345 * to 348 * Failed attempt to recapture Damascus in Syria by Byzantium.
345 * to 348 * Byzantine fleet off Alexandria unsuccessful against the Arabs
Event in Mesopotamia and Persia:
345 * Battle of Nihawend in western Iran between advancing Arabs and retreating Persians [presumably this event falls from the fictional year 642 **, where the Sassanids were finally overthrown, in the future 939 * OR the north Persian tribe of the Bujids (Shiite Muslims) is from Christian chroniclers passed over and is the real conqueror of Persia from 932 * and disempowered the Sassanids at the beginning of the 10th century].
348 Battle of Byzantium against Persia near Singara

348 Siege of Nisito by the Byzantines (see above 338, 346, 350 and 363) against the Persians

----

350 to 351 after Christ:

Event north of the Mediterranean (Romans, Teutons):
350 The Western Roman Emperor Constans is deposed on a hunting excursion in Gaul by the troops of the half-Franconian general Flavius Magnentius in Autun and murdered on the Spanish border.
351 The Eastern Roman Emperor Constantius II defeats Magnentius, who then commits suicide. Constantius II becomes the sole ruler of Rome, albeit without Palestine, Syria, Egypt and Libya, which unofficially have already fallen into Islamic Arab hands.

Event south of the Mediterranean (Arabs):
350 * Arabs reach Tripoli / Libya militarily.
351 * The Arabs are in southern Tunisia and found Subeitala.
[In just under 10 years the eastern North Africa coast will be in Arab hands!]

Event in Mesopotamia and Persia:
since approx. 350 * (+/- 10 years?, i.e. possibly already 340 *) incursion of the Islamized Arabs into Mesopotamia
[Official chronology wants us to believe that the non-existent Huns attacked Persia from the north. They serve the counterfeiters as a substitute for the Arabs who come from the south and whet an appetite for Mesopotamia.]
[Only Armenian and Greek sources report the Huns invading Persia. Here, too, the Persians have no history of their own!]

----

352 to 360 after Christ:

Event north of the Mediterranean (Romans, Teutons):

352 * to 359 battles on land and sea (see under "Arabs" and "Mesopotamia and Persians"), also:
357 wars of the Roman emperor in Spe Julian Apostata against Alemanni and Franks successful near Strasbourg.
358 Wars of Constantius II against Quaden and Sarmatians on the Danube.

Event south of the Mediterranean (Arabs):
352 * New Arab fleet (created with the help of Phoenician engineers) attacks a Roman island for the first time: attack on Cyprus. Tribute payments to the Arabs until approx. 965, when Cyprus was "finally" conquered back by Byzantium. Between 352 * and 965 Arab-Byzantine condominium in Cyprus. (therefore 316 years duration)
355 * First Arabian attack on Sicily, but unsuccessful!
357 * drive to Rhodes; Arabs suddenly return to Alexandria.
356 * to 358 * Arab advance to the Persian Caucasus invented because unrealistic! Because the Arabs are still allies of the Persians. However, if this should mean an attack on Roman Armenia, then it only makes sense in conjunction with the Persians. [The advance in North Africa stalled in Tunisia for 50 years because of Roman Carthage. Hence Arab reserves of Tunisia for attack on Armenia conceivable.]
358 * Naval battle off Finix (near today's Antalya) with victory of the Arab fleet over Ostrom.

Event in Mesopotamia and Persia:
359 The Persian king Shapur II invades Eastern Roman areas. Emperor Constantius wages war against the Persians until his death. [That fits perfectly with the raids of the Arabs in the Caucasus and Armenia in the years 653 ** to 654 **, according to time forgers!]
approx. 360 The Persians make an alliance with the Arabs. Persians and Arabs are now jointly attacking Roman territory. [The time counterfeiters prefer to speak of the fictional "Huns" when talking about their ally of the Persians.]

---
361 to 369 after Christ:

Event north of the Mediterranean (Romans, Teutons):
361 Emperor Constantius II, the last son of Constantine the Great, dies.
from 364 Valentinian I Emperor of Westrom and Valens Emperor of East Rome.
364 to 375 war against the Goths. Victory over the Alemanni 366 in the Catalaunian fields with restoration of the Rhine border.
368 to 369 fights in Britain.

Event south of the Mediterranean (Arabs):
361 * to 369 * the Arabs are busy with internal tasks and undertake next to no attacks. The Romans are only concerned with Teutons, British and Persians in this decade.

Event in Mesopotamia and Persia:
363 Emperor Julian Apostata is killed by his own people in a Persian campaign after the battle of Ctesiphon, which ends with the defeat of the Byzantines. A small part of Armenia with its capital Dvin goes to Persia.

370 to 372 after Christ:

Event north of the Mediterranean (Romans, Teutons):
370 * First Arab attack on Byzantium from the sea fails.
371 francs from the Lower Rhine are settled in Belgium (and thus on Roman territory).

Event south of the Mediterranean (Arabs):
370 * The deceptive calm of the past few years had its reasons: Preparation of an Arab attack on Byzantium from the sea.

372 * Arab advance through Asia Minor without taking possession.

Event in Mesopotamia and Persia:
371 Emperor Valens campaigns in Armenia against the Persians.
[Here a common struggle against Rome / Byzantium can be seen again, hence a year later 372 * the advance of the Arabs to Asia Minor to relieve the Persians OR the Arab advance through Asia Minor is in truth a Persian one.]
----
374 to 375 after Christ:

Event north of the Mediterranean (Romans, Teutons):
374 to 375 Valentinian's Danube War against the Quads; Emperor Valentinian dies. Quads and vandals settle in the Roman province of Pannonia.
375 Victory over the vandals at Aquincum (Budapest) [presumably the vandals will be wiped out here !!!, the attack on the Rhine border approx 25 years later and the march to North Africa, where the Muslim Arabs have been sitting since 370/401, is fictitious !!!]

Event south of the Mediterranean (Arabs):
375 * Founding of Kairuan by the Muslim Arabs (150 km south of Tunis or Carthage)
----
377 to 381 after Christ:

Event north of the Mediterranean (Romans, Teutons):
377 to 378 Emperor Valens is killed in the battle against the Goths near Hadrianopel (north of Byzantium); great defeat of the Byzantines. The Goths have to be settled on imperial territory.

Event south of the Mediterranean (Arabs):

377 * to 381 * First large siege of Byzantium by the Islamized Arabs, for the first time from the sea and land side. [Perhaps the Arabs only attack from the sea side while the Persians support them from the land side.]

377 AD Byzantium is threatened from the north by the Ostrogoths and from the south by the Arabs. If one deliberately tears something like that apart for 297 years, then one believes in far too great powers and possibilities of the Ostrogoths. What exactly happened in detail and in what order can no longer be determined too precisely afterwards. Were the Ostrogoths allied with the Arabs (and Persians?) And then with the Byzantines after making massive concessions? In any case, Constantinople was involved in a two-front war for the first time right outside its own city walls, exactly 40 years after Constantine the Great's death!

Event in Mesopotamia and Persia:
377 * to 381 * Participation of the Persians in the siege of Byzantium?
----
388 and 394 after Christ just in Rome:

Event north of the Mediterranean (Romans, Teutons):
Civil war battles 388, 394. Internal battles of Rome. The external enemies let their weapons rest for 20 years. Emperor Theodosius, father of the two successors Arcadius (Byzantium) and Honorius (Rome), declared Christianity to be the state religion. That he should have forbidden paganism in Egypt is pure nonsense, because the land on the Nile has belonged since 345 * AD no longer to Rome, but to the Islamized Arabs (and Persians?).

Event south of the Mediterranean (Arabs):
The Arabs can no longer keep up the pace of the conquests. After the break from 361 * to 370 *, there is another rest phase from 381 * to 401 *.

---

401 after Christ

Event north of the Mediterranean (Romans, Teutons):
401 Invasion of the Visigoths under Alaric in northern Italy (coming from Croatia).
401 Picten and Scoten, coming from Scotland, storm Hadrian's Wall in northern England and conquer areas as far as Central England.

Event south of the Mediterranean (Arabs):
401 * Fall of Carthage! After the invasion of northern Italy by the Visigoths, the Roman troops had to be withdrawn from the city of Carthage in northern Tunisia, which had been besieged by the Arabs since 375 *, because Rome is now directly threatened by the Visigoths.

---

402 to 410 after Christ (Rome's End is not far):

Event north of the Mediterranean (Romans, Teutons):
410 Rome is for the first time since 387 BC. (after 797 years !!!) conquered again by a strange people!
After two defensive battles by the Romans under Stilicho 402 and 403 near Verona and Pollenca, the city is helplessly at the mercy of the Visigoths under Alaric.
410 The Romans leave England for good.

Event south of the Mediterranean (Arabs):
402 * to 410 * The Arabs advance as far as Algeria and Morocco.

Event in Mesopotamia and Persia:
408 * Official advance of the Arabs beyond Persia (Bukhara and Samarkand) and into the Indus Valley, pure invention. (It is possible that the Persians themselves took such actions under the Sassanids.)

---

412 to 414 after Christ

Event north of the Mediterranean (Romans, Teutons):
412 After the death of Alaric, the new king of the Visigoths, Athaulf, moves to the south of France.

Event south of the Mediterranean (Arabs):
414 * The Arabs cross the Strait near Gibraltar and, coming from Morocco, invade Spain for the first time.

----

415 after Christ

Event north of the Mediterranean (Romans, Teutons):
In 415 Athaulf dies as king of the Visigoths. Officially for a blood revenge. A war injury in the fight against the Muslim Arabs is also conceivable.

Event south of the Mediterranean (Arabs):
415 * Arabs conquer Toledo.
Thus, only a) because of the Visigoths the extreme north-east of Spain is unoccupied, b) the extreme north-west of Spain because of the mountain peoples there, who were able to maintain their independence for a long time since the Roman times, and c) because of the remains of Roman troops, the extreme south-west between Nova Karthagena and Alicante. This Roman territory can be held until 459 *. The Balearic Islands fell to Islam in 501 *.
The advance of the Arabs in Spain (on the river Ebro) in 415 * was finally stopped by the alliance between the Visigoths and the Romans. The Battle of Poitiers 435 * is a pure invention. Even some historians who do not belong to the circle of chronology critics doubt this battle.

----

420 to 423 after Christ

Event north of the Mediterranean (Romans, Teutons):
420 * to 421 * Siege of Byzantium by Arabs (and Persians?).

420 to 421 Rome's fight against Persia for persecuting Christians in Persia. [Pure invention of Christian historians to divert attention from the siege of Byzantium by the Arabs. Because the time from 614 to 911 does not exist, one or the other military action will have to be agreed. A relief attack on Persia (and the Arabs) is at most possible.]

Event south of the Mediterranean (Arabs):
423 The Arabs conquer western Sicily

---

429 to 443 after Christ

Event north of the Mediterranean (Romans, Teutons):
429 * to 443 * annual raids by the Arabs (or Persians?) Into Asia Minor.
441 Invasion of Roman territory by the Persians because the annual tribute payments by the Romans to the Persians did not materialize. Allegedly, the Romans paid small amounts of tribute as aid against the Huns who invaded Persia. [If you put the history of the Arabs back 297 years to 911, then you can clearly see an alliance between Arabs and Persians in the struggle in Asia Minor. As already written, the Huns are a pure invention to cover up the phantom time.]
443 The Burgundians migrate from the Rhine to today's Burgundy.

Event in Mesopotamia and Persia:
429 * to 443 * annual raids by the Arabs (or Persians?) Into Asia Minor.

---

450 to 465 after Christ

Event north of the Mediterranean (Romans, Teutons):
450 Angling, Saxons and Jutes emigrate to England.
In 455 the Vandals officially attacked the city of Rome from Carthage (Tunisia). The Germanic people, however, were wiped out on the Danube as early as 375 [noble vandals

91

were perhaps even sold to Tunisia at that time]. If this probable attack on Rome was "by sea," then it was certainly carried out by the Arabs from Carthage. A first attack across the Mediterranean is almost overdue after the sister city of Byzantium has already been exposed to this type of attack several times. In contrast to the city on the Bosporus, the municipality on the Tiber can hardly defend itself.

Event south of the Mediterranean (Arabs):
455 Attack of the Arabs (presumably the Vandals only talked about in North Africa) on Rome from sea.
458/459 * The Umayyad Abdarrahman founds the emirate of Cordoba in Spain. Shortly before, the Romans lost their last two bases, Nova Carthage and Alicante in Spain. This means that only the extreme north of the Iberian Peninsula is not in Islamic hands.

Event in Mesopotamia and Persia:
465 * The Arabs let the village of Baghdad (Persian: God's gift) grow into a city, make it their residence and maintain a lively cultural exchange with the Persians. [The weight of Arab politics is shifting from Rome to the "former" ally Persia.]
465 Sasanids suffer a crushing defeat against the fictional Huns. [So against the Arabs, because a) the conquest of the Arabs against Rome has been greatly slowed down, ie only small bases and islands will be conquered in the future and the Arabs have "time for the Persians", and b) the sources refer to "minus 297 years "in Arabia that the village of Baghdad grows into a city precisely in 465 * by the Arabs.] This means that Baghdad was not founded peacefully, but warlike by the Arabs on Persian territory.
----
467 to 476 after Christ

Event north of the Mediterranean (Romans, Teutons):

92

476 The last Roman emperor Augustulus (puppet of the Teutons and Byzantines) is deposed.

Event in Mesopotamia and Persia:
467 Diplomatic settlement of a dispute between Romans and Persians. Furthermore, around 450 because of the uprising of Christian Armenians, no diplomatic interference by the Romans in Persia and around 480 financial support from the Romans to the Persians officially against the fictitious Hephalites (Huns), unofficially against probably the Arabs. [Due to the Arab founding of Baghdad on the territory of the Persian kings from the house of the Sassanids, a Persian change of alliance from Arabia to Rome could exist here in 467.]

----

482 to 499 after Christ

Event north of the Mediterranean (Romans, Teutons):
482 The Franks found their empire in France
493 Ostrogoths found their empire in Italy

Event south of the Mediterranean (Arabs):

Event in Mesopotamia and Persia:
In 484 the Sassanids suffer another major defeat against the fictional Huns [that is, against the Arabs].
484 to about 540: The Persians owe tribute to the fictional Huns [in truth to the Arabs].
498/499 Interference of the fictional Huns [i.e. Arabs] in the Sassanid controversies for the throne.

Event in Northern and Eastern Europe (Vikings, Hungarians, Slavs):
496 * Vikings destroy Lindisfarne Monastery in Northern England.

----

501 to 507 after Christ

Event north of the Mediterranean (Romans, Teutons):
507 The Franconian King Clovis I destroys the last Visigoth king Alaric II.

Event south of the Mediterranean (Arabs):
501 The Balearic Islands are conquered by the Arabs.

----

508 to 526 after Christ

Event north of the Mediterranean (Romans, Teutons):
508 to 526 The Ostrogoth king Theodoric the Great ruled from Ravenna in Italy, Pannonia (Croatia etc.) and the coast to Marseille.

These are happy years in northern Italy and elsewhere in the Mediterranean. There is no fighting on any front in these almost 20 years. Perhaps that is why the mausoleum of Theodoric in Ravenna exudes an overwhelming peaceful calm, which carries its vibrations far into the distance. -----

----

526 to 542 after Christ

Event north of the Mediterranean (Romans, Teutons):
526 to 540 unofficially possibly peaceful handover (inheritance?) Of Italy from Ostrogoths to Justinian I and Byzantium [officially belligerent]. As a result, Sardinia and Corsica were lost to the Arabs. Theodora, wife of Justinian, possibly because of the name, daughter of Theodoric the Great.
532 The Burgundy empire is finally destroyed by the Merovingians.

Event south of the Mediterranean (Arabs):
530 * Sardinia and Crete become Arabic.
[The Arabs militarily secure part of the Ostrogoths' legacy. The mainland of Italy and Corsica, on the other hand, is completely transferred to the Byzantines, who want to trump

the splendor of the Arab and Persian architecture, e.g. in Cordoba, with their buildings in Ravenna.]

Event in Mesopotamia and Persia:
531 to 579 Under the reign of the legendary Chosrau I, the Persian Empire was able to move away from Arab influences (and thus also from Islam).
531 & 562 Alliances of Persia with Byzantium. The traditional attack on Palestine and Syria by Chosrau from 540 onwards is not directed against the Romans, but against the Arabs. A blow against the Arabs there is possible in order to free themselves from the obligation to pay tribute.

Event in Northern and Eastern Europe (Vikings, Hungarians, Slavs):
542 * The Vikings attack Dublin, Ireland.
----
547 to around 560 after Christ

Event south of the Mediterranean (Arabs):
553 * Corsica becomes Arabic. [A weak phase of the Byzantines is exploited]

Event in Mesopotamia and Persia:
around 560 In an alliance between the Western Turks and Persia, the Huns are said to be defeated [in fact, more likely the Islamized Arabs].
Event in Northern and Eastern Europe (Vikings, Hungarians, Slavs):
547 * and 550 * The Vikings make forays off the coast of southern Spain and thereby harass the Arabs. In addition, Bordeaux in France is besieged.
----
568 to 579 after Christ

Event north of the Mediterranean (Romans, Teutons):

568 Alliance of the Turks with the Byzantines against the Persians. [The Turks change fronts. To what extent and how the Arabs are involved here is unclear.]

Event in Mesopotamia and Persia:
579 Chorau I. dies. After his death there is new turmoil and controversy over the throne. After two regents, Chorau II comes to power from 590 to 628.

Event in Northern and Eastern Europe (Vikings, Hungarians, Slavs):
569 * The Vikings launch an oversized pincer attack on Europe. On the one hand, they repeatedly threaten the coasts of England, France and Spain. On the other hand, they come to the Black Sea via Kiev in the Ukraine and lay siege to Byzantium.
567 Exactly two years before the Vikings reach Byzantium, the Avars emigrate from the Ukraine to Hungary and the Bulgarians from there to today's Bulgaria. They are driven west by the Vikings.
[It is obvious that if 297 years are subtracted, these two events coincide exactly.]

581 to around 600 after Christ

Event north of the Mediterranean (Romans, Teutons):
2nd half of the 6th century. The Franks invade northern Italy and secure rule over the peninsula as far as Rome. Roman citizenship was suspended at the end of the 6th century. From now on only the high clergy and the aristocracy have comparable rights. The south remains in Byzantine hands. Corsica and Sardinia remain with the Arabs. Sicily is still fiercely contested between Byzantium and Islam.
2nd half of the 6th century * Because Ravenna is no longer safe enough, Venice is founded in a lagoon. Christianity has the year 600 AD the heaviest test ahead. The building of the

96

city is a preventive measure used by wealthy Romans. It was able to maintain its independence until the time of Napoleon Bonaparte.

Event south of the Mediterranean (Arabs):
In 581 one of the numerous raids by the Arabs on Sicily occurs again. In contrast to Sardinia and Corsica, Sicily cannot be conquered in one piece. The resistance is so fierce that the island can only be completely taken for some time after the first attack 200 years later. The last Christian base does not fall until 924 (around 40 years after 581). As early as 423, Sicily was attacked for the first time by the Arabs through Tunisia.

Event in Northern and Eastern Europe (Vikings, Hungarians, Slavs):
2nd half of the 6th century * The Vikings continue to attack the coasts of Germany, France and Spain.
2nd half of the 6th century * The Slavs immigrate to depopulated areas in the Balkans. Like the Avars and Bulgarians from 567 * onwards, they were probably driven to the west by the Ukrainian Vikings.
598 * The Hungarians also immigrate to the Hungarian lowlands. [However, it is not entirely clear whether the Hungarians are not identical with the Avars, so that the Hungarians, expelled by the Vikings, migrated to the Tisza and Balaton in 567 *.]

----

614 = 911 (same year) after Christ

JUMP FROM 8/31/614 to 9/1/911 the next day!

Event in Northern and Eastern Europe (Vikings, Hungarians, Slavs):
911 Both in Normandy (France) and in the Ukraine around Kiev the Viking states are founded and this is confirmed by Greek-Byzantine treaties.

---

925 to 955 after Christ

Event north of the Mediterranean (Romans, Teutons):
From 600 to 950 [50 years] Byzantines control the papacy.

Event in Mesopotamia and Persia:
925 * After the death of Chosrau II, another chaotic time begins. Countless murders and regents take turns.
929/30 * to 948 * The last Persian and non-Islamic great king reigns as Yazdegerd III.
932 to 949 The Persian Bujids (on the Caspian Sea around Tehran) conquered Persia and ended the rule of the Sassanids.
934 * The Persian palace in Ctesiphon (Iraq) is destroyed by the attacking Arabs.
948 * Yazdegerd III. is killed while fleeing in the northeast of his empire.

It is not the Arabs that are militarily spreading Islam in Persia, but rather an ethnic group of the Persians who have converted to Islam themselves. The fact that Tehran will become the new capital of Persia is only a logical consequence of this fact.
Event in Northern and Eastern Europe (Vikings, Hungarians, Slavs):
924 The Hungarians invade Thuringia.
from approx. 920 The Slavs advance peacefully to Croatia.
955 The Hungarians are defeated by German troops on the Lechfeld near Augsburg and finally pushed back into present-day Hungary.

---

961 to 975 after Christ

Event north of the Mediterranean (Romans, Teutons):
961 The Byzantines recapture Crete.
965 The Byzantines recapture Cyprus.

969 The Byzantines retake Antioch.
975 A Byzantine invasion of Lebanon is repulsed by the Arabs.
Second half of the 10th century. Corsica can be recaptured with the combined forces of the Franks, Romans and Byzantines.

Event south of the Mediterranean (Arabs):
965 The last Christian base in Sicily falls to the Arabs from Tunisia. This means that every square kilometer of the island is now in Islamic hands.
975 The southern French base of the Arabs Fraxinetum is recaptured by the Franks, the Romans and the Byzantines.

Event in Mesopotamia and Persia:

Event in Northern and Eastern Europe (Vikings, Hungarians, Slavs):
971 With a victory against the Bulgarians in what is now Bulgaria, the Vikings keep the people away from the city of Byzantium.
----
980 to 989 after Christ
Event in Mesopotamia and Persia:
Around 980, a famous Persian poet pays homage to his sultan, but without mentioning the Koran.

Event in Northern and Eastern Europe (Vikings, Hungarians, Slavs):
989 The Vikings in Kiev convert to Christianity.

Annual rings – C14 – moon – no linearity

Hans-Erdmann Korth wrote in Oct. 2013 (among many other things) in his book "Der Größte Irrtum der Weltgeschichte":
"As an experimental physicist, I had learned to clarify technical facts. Meaningful measurement data obtained with the help of suitable experimental setups provided me with the answers I was looking for. If Illig's strange thesis was wrong, that was immediately clear to me, then this would be easy to prove: A large number of wood samples from historical times, on which the age as well as the number of years that had passed since their formation could be determined on the basis of the C14 content and the annual rings, had been examined. If there was an approximately linear relationship between their age and the year count, then Illig's thesis was disproved - briefly and painlessly. Barely two years later - at that time the topic history did not seem to me to be such a priority - I came back to this consideration and got the data of the calibration curve for the radiocarbon age freely available on the Internet. This so-called IntCal curve serves to convert age values determined with the help of C14 measurements to the year numbers of the dendrochronology. Over thousands of years, the measured values actually follow a straight line quite well. To my astonishment, however, only up to the Middle Ages. Extended to the present, they appear offset by three centuries - just as one would expect from Illig's thesis! The peculiar course of the curve was explained by H. Suess with fluctuations of the ratio of radioactive carbon atoms (C14 and stable C12) in the atmosphere, which led to decades of dispute with the discoverer W. Libby."

"IntCal stands for International Calibration and represents the current consensus of scientists concerned with radiocarbon (C14). The data were last revised in 2008 (IntCal09), before that IntCal04 and IntCal98 were valid."

On his website (see the end of the book) Adalbert Feltz mentions the American physicist and astronomer Robert Russel Newton (1918-1991), who has analyzed solar and lunar eclipses over the past 3000 years. The moon moves about 4 cm away from the earth per year and it slows down. There is an irregularity between 500 and 1000 AD. If you equate 614 with 911, then this disappears. A Werner Frank could demonstrate this, according to Feltz.

Remark 2021: This chapter is not in either of my two books, it is completely new.

The Turks

The first time the Turks appear in the Persian area is in 575 AD, when they attacked eastern Persia as allies of the Byzantines. Shortly before, the Turks may have served as allies to the Byzantines against the Vikings. Perhaps also against the Arabs attacking from the sea.
The Persians counterattack the Byzantines over the decades by integrating captured Turks into their forces as war slaves. In Persian service, the Turks rise socially in Persia. This occurs as early as the beginning of the 10th century, just a few decades after 575.
Approximately 200 years after 575, therefore in the year 1075, the Turks defeat a Byzantine army at Lake Van or at Manzikert in the east of today's Turkcy and stand a few years later directly in front of Constantinople (=Byzantium =Istanbul). Here now the first crusade was necessary or the Mongol storm in the 13th century, which saved Byzantium the ancient existence until 1453 AD.

Byzantium is looking for new allies

After the Persians had cleverly taken over first the Arabs from about 337 AD (presumption: joint fight against Rome, provision of auxiliary troops under Arab command and aid money) and then the Turks from about 920 AD (i.e. about 300 years later) for their interests, the Byzantines were forced to look for new allies.

They found them in the Russians and the Vikings in the Ukraine. In order not to lose allies to Islam again, it was necessary to make Christianity look better than Islam.
After Constantine the Great (coming from today's Serbia) had declared Jerusalem the center of Christianity, and shortly after his death the Islamized Arabs had conquered the city, Byzantium had to reach into the bag of tricks to woo the Russians (and to keep away the Persians) and to invent time of about 300 years for it.

It is astonishing, if the otherwise so time-exact Greeks and/or Byzantines now suddenly fall back on old-Egyptian techniques, in order to put the own government and world view in substantially better light. The events in Egypt during the times of the pharaohs are artificially pushed further into the past. This creates room for aliens.

Sources in Persia

The history of the Persians and Arabs between 620 and 1000 is documented almost exclusively by Byzantine, Armenian, Christian authors. Many historians point out.

In Arabia and Persia, people probably always had a different understanding of recording historical events for posterity.

The Christian time falsifiers could not know, however, that the Mongols in the 13th century would completely destroy the libraries of the Persians once again. Even before that, there will have been nothing of historical value in Persian libraries.

But if the Christian chroniclers succeeded in deceiving Arabs and Persians between 317 and 911, then it can be assumed that both peoples were strangers to precise historiography.

Certainly, Persians can be assumed to migrate to Arabia, just as Arabs migrated to Persia. Especially the period from 317 to 1000 is interesting here. But these movements of population masses were described – as far as I read – again only by Christian chroniclers and are therefore manipulable in their sense.

Thus one can invent regents in Persia between 614 and 911, which did not exist at all. In Arabia exactly the traditional ones existed, only these did not live between 614 and 911, but between 317 and 614.

Illig and other chronology critics

There are several authors who argue in popular science books that certain sections of the chronology and historiography are incorrect due to errors and deliberate forgery. The following is taken verbatim from Wikipedia:

Immanuel Velikovsky

The Russian psychoanalyst Immanuel Velikovsky (1895–1979) became known as the founder of neocatastrophism and also dealt with the history of ancient Egypt. He reconstructed this assuming a temporal coincidence of the exodus of the people of Israel with the catastrophe described in the papyrus, among other things. As a result, he shortened the passage of time around the Middle Kingdom (see also David Rohl). Since all ancient chronologies are based on the Egyptian, the shortening leads to the deletion of around 550 years from the conventional chronology. He also followed the approach that "dark centuries" were a mistake in historiography and should be viewed as fiction. His work is summarized in the Ages in Chaos series. They were translated into German by the Swiss Christoph Marx. Marx assumes that there have been catastrophes in historical times, these have been suppressed, which is why mainstream historiography comes to wrong judgments. In this, Marx follows Velikovsky's catastrophism, which he also knew personally. He formulated the thesis of a "last big jolt" in the Trecento and describes the Holocaust and wars as repetitive rituals that are supposed to be based on the suppression of this catastrophe. He wants to explain the errors in the Julian calendar by shifting the earth's axis. These theses contradict scientific knowledge and fundamentally differ from Heribert Illig's phantom time thesis. Marx rejects the established scientific methodology as part of the "repression apparatus" and declares any genuine history to be impossible. Velikowsky, on the other hand, believed at the time in a reconstruction with the help of conventional history.

Anatoli Fomenko

The mathematician Anatoli Fomenko (* 1945) believes that, through statistical analysis of historical source material from antiquity and the Middle Ages, he can prove that the same stories were composed in different forms in different epochs and thus repeated, since numerous ruling dynasties and events (e.g. Wars) should show conspicuous and statistically significant parallels in other epochs. So be inter alia. the Almagest of Claudius Ptolemy was not made until around the year 1000 and thus the time of Jesus was only about 1000 years ago. From this he developed his New Chronology. Like the majority of modern chronology critics, Fomenko questioned the objective methods of dating age, such as B. Dendrochronology and radiocarbon dating. Fomenko found support from, among others, Eugen Gabowitsch and the former Russian chess world champion and current politician Garri Kasparow. Igor Davidenko and Yaroslav Kesler continued Fomenko's approach. In their attempts at reconstruction, Uwe Topper and Christoph Marx also referred to Fomenko's criticism and his method of statistical text analysis.

Wilhelm Kammeier

The former elementary school teacher Wilhelm Kammeier (1889-1959) is the originator of the thesis of the "invented Middle Ages", which he developed in the 1920s and published in book form in 1935. His main argument was the allegedly proven late forgery of all medieval documents and manuscripts. Kammeier wrote three other chronology-critical books. In the 1990s, his thesis was taken up by the Germanist Heribert Illig (* 1945) and the non-fiction author Uwe Topper (* 1940) and promoted in the media.

Heribert Illig – Gunnar Heinsohn – Hans-Ulrich Niemitz

In his work, first published in 1994, Heribert Illig postulates that the time between the 7th and 10th centuries AD was inserted into the chronology by forgeries by Ottonian historians and that Charlemagne never existed. In addition, Illig worked together with the sociologist Gunnar Heinsohn (* 1943) on the Egyptian chronology, whereby, in contrast to Velikovsky, they do not only rely on biblical sources. Heinsohn agreed with Illig's phantom time thesis and tried to check it against the Carolus and Pippin coins. He came to the conclusion that all Carolus coins should come from Charles the Simple and that the Carolingian coin reform went back to Pippin the Elder. Heinsohn also believes he can prove that the Sumerians never existed and that the history of Mesopotamia and Egypt was allegedly stretched by 2000 years to support the biblical story. The technical historian Hans-Ulrich Niemitz (1946 - 2010) supports, like Illig, the theory of an invented period of time in the early Middle Ages (the term phantom years comes from him) and in his book fundamentally doubts the reliability of radiocarbon dating and dendrochronology as well as all other scientific dating methods.

Uwe Topper

Uwe Topper (* 1940) is one of the most journalistic history critics in German-speaking countries and has written several books on this subject. He expanded Illig's thesis and assumed that Mohammed lived about 297 years earlier and thus the emergence of Islam (622) coincided with the condemnation of Arius at the Council of Nicaea in 325. Later, Topper's publications tended towards Fomenko's 1000-year theory. Like him, he claims that all documents of non-European historiography, for example from India and China, are relatively recent forgeries. Another controversial thesis of Topper is the view that the Hurrites (whom he called Horra) played a central role in the Copper Age. Like other chronology critics, Topper doubts the established picture of earth's history and Darwin's theory of evolution.

Hans-Joachim Zillmer

The graduate engineer Hans-Joachim Zillmer (* 1950) tries, like Fomenko and Topper, to prove that the antiquity we know only began about 1000 years ago and was projected far into the past through falsified historiography and increased by means of similar repetitions. Zillmer comes to the conclusion that the Roman Empire never existed in Rome, but that the real Romans were on the one hand Etruscans who founded Rome, and on the other hand represented ancient Greeks who ruled south of Etruria also in southern Italy and Sicily (Magna Graecia). Zillmer suspects a major natural disaster ("Little Ice Age") in the 6th century as the reason for the break in history. Zillmer shares Illig's view that three centuries (7th-9th centuries) should be deleted from history. He also denies the existence of the Ice Age; instead it assumes a much shorter "snow time". In various reviews of his books, Zillmer's theses were consistently rejected as scientifically untenable.

Horst Friedrich

In his book "Jahrhundert-Irrtum Eiszeit" from 1997, the philosopher of science Horst Friedrich doubts the current notions about the ice ages. He claims that glaciers hundreds of kilometers in length never existed, and that glaciers could not possibly have transported boulders over such long distances because they lacked the necessary "thrust". Friedrich's theses are considered untenable by natural scientists and all of them have been refuted.

Roland P. Mayer

The author Roland P. Mayer has added another variant to the chronology criticism in two books, both self-published. He assumes that the Byzantine Empire was the only great power of the late antiquity and the Middle Ages from which all cultural impulses had come. The Roman-German Empire had been only a satellite state. In the Byzantine Empire, the Arian and Greek Orthodox churches existed as state churches with equal rights, while the Catholic Church was only invented later. Mayer justifies this thesis with the fact that the cult of Mithras, which was widespread in late antique Rome, was at first the actual state religion and then, after the conquest by Byzantium, was exchanged for the very similar Christian faith of the Arian type - which proves the hegemonic position of Byzantium. Mayer sees an important prerequisite for his assumptions in Illig's phantom period theory, since he could use it to erase Charlemagne's imperial coronation independent of Byzantium, which would contradict his thesis. Illig, however, has distanced himself from Mayer's thesis. Mayer himself admits that his speculations cannot be based on sources, since no written evidence of the alleged rule of Byzantine officials in Western Europe has survived.

Eugen Gabowitsch

The mathematician Eugen Gabowitsch (1938-2009 considered the chronology of China to be false and held the view that the Great Wall of China was mainly built only in the 20th century. From Gabowitsch comes the aperçu: "The greatest falsification in the history of mankind is the history of mankind".

Gernot L. Geise - Georg Menting

Gernot L. Geise, in his 2002 book The Irreality of the Roman Empire - Who Were the Romans Really? questions the common ideas about the Roman Empire. He is a founding member and on the board of Efodon e. V. ("European Society for Early Historical Technology and Marginal Areas of Science") and, together with Horst Friedrich, edits its journal "Efodon-Synesis." With lectures, essays and a book Georg Menting has made his theses known since 1998, which also met with approval in creationist circles.

Christoph Pfister

The historian Christoph Pfister (* 1945) is one of the most far-reaching advocates of the chronology critique. According to Pfister, both the history of the earth and the history of civilization must be radically shortened. He disputes the reliability of any scientific age dating. Earth-historically he is a supporter of the neo-catastrophism. Pfister believes to have to shorten the entire human history since the earliest advanced civilizations in his book to less than 1000 years: He considers the ancient cultures of the Celts, Greeks and Romans to be Renaissance inventions. In his opinion, the Pantheon in Rome dates from the 16th century, which Pfister regards as the actual Middle Ages. Hebrew, he says, is a religious art language that also was not invented until the 16th century, along with the Bible and all other ancient writings. All history before 1600, he says, is a forgery and invention of early modern scholars Joseph Justus Scaliger and Denis Pétau.

Gerard Serrade

With his book "Empty Times - or: The Abstract Image of History" Gerard Serrade is considered one of the most radical critics of chronology. His thesis is: All dating before

1582 (Gregorian calendar reform) is wrong. Our history is only an abstract construction of the historians.

Zoltán Hunnivári

Zoltán Hunnivári postulates in his works that the time between 960 and 1160 AD was inserted. Therefore, the popes and the corresponding emperors of that time are also pure invention. After its time calculation system, the "Hungarian calendar" was introduced the Julian calendar 154 o.c. and the birth of Jesus Christ occurred in the year 194 o.c. Its first book appeared in the year 2002 in Hungarian language. Later, an edition in English followed in 2004 and in German in 2008 with the title "Revolution in Chronology - 200 Years of Time Shift".

Very special attention from critics of chronology research gets the most famous researcher, Dr. Illig:

Heribert Illig

from Wikipedia, the free encyclopedia
Switch to: Navigation, Search
Heribert Illig (born 1947 in Vohenstrauß in Bavaria) is a German publicist and publisher who has become known as a chronology critic.
Illig studied German and received his doctorate with a thesis on Egon Friedell. In other books, Illig has edited Friedell's work in part and commented on it in part. He worked as a systems analyst for a bank before devoting himself full-time to his publishing activities.
From 1981 to 1988, Illig was a leading member of the Society for the Reconstruction of Human and Natural History. He edited the journal "Vorzeit-Frühzeit-Gegenwart" from 1989 to 1994 and is editor of the journal "Zeitensprünge", which

grew out of it. He is also the owner of Mantis-Verlag in Gräfelfing, which publishes this journal and books by Illig and Gunnar Heinsohn, among others.

For many years, his works have focused on chronological criticism. In doing so, he first turned to early history. Together with Heinsohn, Illig also worked on the history of ancient Egypt, for which they propose a reduction of two thousand years. Accordingly, the construction of the Cheops pyramid would fall into the first pre-Christian millennium as well as the megalithic culture. This would shorten the distances to the Old Stone Age as well as to the cave paintings of that time among themselves into the millennium range.

For the Middle Ages Illig put 1991 the more well-known thesis that 297 years of the historiography in the period September 614 to August 911 would not have taken place. Illig calls this time the invented Middle Ages (occasionally also: phantom time).

Illig's theses on chronology criticism received media attention primarily in popular science publications and the daily press. They were rejected by historians as unscientific, among other things, with reference to methodological errors and described as scientifically refuted.

After Illig's publication of the book "Das erfundene Mittelalter" (The Invented Middle Ages) in 1996 by Econ Verlag, its contents were the subject of scholarly interest and attracted attention in several reviews.

As early as April 1996, Johannes Fried commented in the "Historische Zeitschrift," affirming the existence of Charlemagne's son by pointing to simultaneous and independent accounts appearing in many sources and calling Illig's thesis "a misleading, inadmissible illusion."

On October 1, 1996, Matthias Gräßlin commented on Illig's book in the Frankfurter Allgemeine Zeitung, pointing out that there was no evidence for Illig's thesis, that it was based on questionable methods, and that it was "historically worthless."

In 1997, Illig presented several statements of his thesis on the invention of the early Middle Ages for discussion in the journal Ethics and Social Sciences. Illig's statements on the Invented Middle Ages were considered by experts from different historical directions:

- Gerd Althoff shows that an advanced civilization with all its facets would have had to be invented if Illig was right and calls Illig's thesis an "abstruse idea". Furthermore, Althoff presents the enormous falsification effort that would have been necessary to make Illig's thesis coherent. Althoff concludes that the forgery of the Middle Ages postulated by Illig is impossible.
- Werner Bergmann looks at Illig's thesis in relation to computistics and calculates the effects of the Gregorian calendar reform on the Easter date set for the Council of Nicaea. In doing so, he shows that, contrary to Illig's assertion, there is no time missing.
- Michael Borgolte examines Illig's approach, which was similar to 19th century positivist thinking. was arrested. Illig overlooks the historical scientific knowledge that all facts can never be collected completely, and that these facts do not allow knowledge from themselves, but only in connection with other facts. For this reason, Borgolte also criticizes Illig's offense at all early medieval incidents, which apparently remained without analogies in your time. Borgolte comes to the conclusion that Illig's approaches are "methodologically flawed and scientifically problematic".
- According to Helmut Flachenecker, Illig is assuming a conspiracy thesis, but without specifying the conspirators and the purpose of the conspiracy. Illig also lacks other sources that can substantiate his thesis. Illig's thesis would therefore only remain "scientific self-abandonment". Flachenecker criticizes Illig's belief in

progress and hubris, which is shown in Illig's flawed premise of a straightforward story that Illig's thesis should be rejected because of its weakness in history theory.

- Gunnar Heinsohn considers "a careful examination of Illig's thesis inevitable" and suggests that Illig's thesis should be checked on the basis of excavations in cities with an assumed continuity of settlement between 600 and 900. He also gives further examples according to which written sources are said to have decreased between 500 and 800 and sees Illig's thesis as a solution for dating the life dates of Moses von Choren. In addition, Heinsohn speculates about possible motives for the forgery postulated by Illig.

- Theo Kölzer completely rejects a discussion of Illig's theses because of their absurdity.

- Like Werner Bergmann, Dietrich Lohrmann proves Illig's incorrect calculation approach for the Gregorian calendar reform. He falsifies Illig's claim that the building of the Aachen Palatine Chapel was unconditional and showed Illig deficiencies in the interpretation of written sources, especially in Latin. Lohrmann criticizes that Illig did not deal with the legacies of the time Illig questioned and that he mainly dealt with secondary literature.

- Jan van der Meulen deals in detail with Illig's architectural-historical arguments and rejects them.
  Wolfhard Schlosser checks the consistency of Illig's theses on the basis of historically known astronomical events and comes to the conclusion that Illig's thesis is not tenable from an astronomical point of view.
  Also in 1997, the then magazine of the Association of History Teachers dealt with Illig's theses in science and teaching.

- Hartmut Boockmann commented on Illig in the editorial and describes Illig's book as "obviously nonsensical" and refers to Wilhelm Kammeier, a predecessor of Illig, who viewed the entire Middle Ages as the product of a forgery.

113

- Rudolf Schieffer wrote in the same magazine and showed Illig numerous methodological errors.

In 1997 Richard Herzinger attested to the public a "need to rewrite and reinterpret history", which Illig served. Herzinger explains that Illig shows historical science that the interpretation of the past is largely based on conceptual constructions and not on clearly verifiable facts. Herzinger complains that Illig proceeds in the same way with his thesis Ekkehard Eickhoff pointed out in a review of the follow-up volume "Who turned the clock" published by Illig in 1999 to the enormous effort that would have required a falsification of history postulated by Illig.
Michael Borgolte already sees the scientific debate about Illig's thesis as concluded in 1999.
Stephan Matthiesen dealt with Illig's thesis in the journal Der Skeptiker in 2001 and also sheds light on the reactions of scientists to Illig's thesis. In doing so, he states that "in fact, several historians have commented on his theses in a well-founded and detailed but clear manner"; but no further argument.

Conclusion of the author of this book:

Overall, all chronology researchers are refuted, by whatever means. One has the impression that even after the abolition of Christianity, the ambiguities in the transition from antiquity to the Middle Ages are no longer cleared. A power does nothing to the preceding one to such an extent. So the truth is only reserved for a small group and the crowd annoys with their insensitivity to exact history. The critics may even know better, but are still stuck in the previous historiography, for whatever reasons. Everyone will be able to imagine different.

Makes Charlemagne megalomaniac

Charlemagne is the father who saved the Christian West in its worst need. Except that this dire misery was not around 790 AD, but around 614 = 911 AD has occurred.
One could compare his charisma with that of Lower Saxony Otto the Great (+963).
Charlemagne has to serve for everything. It is allowed to slaughter a people like the (Lower) Saxons and at the same time they are canonized. Anyone wondering about something like that doesn't have to, because the man didn't even exist. It's like the Vandals and the Huns here. Much useless is then added to inventions.

The danger with Charlemagne is that there are rulers who think that with good training they can fight against any superior force militarily. For some Central European rulers only the fictional Charlemagne reason enough to take it recklessly with a superior force to fight on many fronts at the same time.

Could that have happened a little in 1618, even more so during the Seven Years' War and especially in 1914?

There could be other reasons.

The excessive trust in advisors 1618/19 and 1914 could result from the double occurrence of a special constellation. However, the samples are far too small to be able to derive anything.

Mongol storm: similar with Arabs?

The speed of the conquests, a comparison. How did it work with the Mongols?

Between 1204 and 1206 the tribes in Mongolia are unified and the attack on the neighboring lands begins. Genghis Khan comes to the Caspian Sea by 1220.
Forty years later, the Arabs repel an attack by the Mongols in 1260, but Baghdad is lost in 1258. Around 1240 there is an advance on the Ukraine. Despite victories in Hungary and Silesia, the Mongols withdraw to Ukraine because of the ruler's death. In 1243 the Mongols weaken the Turks on the peninsula of Asia Minor. Only a small strip in northern Iraq on the Caspian Sea is not conquered by the Mongols, it is only dependent. Where the Bujids come from.

These huge areas of conquest by the Mongols in the 13th century could also make a double attack by the Arabs in the 7th century on Palestine, North Africa and Persia possible.

In contrast to the Arab conquests in the alleged 7th century, the Mongolian ones seem to me to be realistic in their speed and spaciousness. However, hardly anyone has put forward a conspiracy theory here. What if the Mongols have not conquered the world at this speed and the written traditions deliberately lead us to believe that the speed is so high as to make the Arab speed too plausible?

On the other hand, it is known that Persia in particular is relatively easy to completely conquer if it no longer has a strong ruler and a power willing to conquer unrestrainedly invades these areas from outside.

After all, the Mongols could be stopped off Asia Minor, off Central Europe and in Syria.

They then broke into China around 1280 and took the Chinese imperial throne.

So after the unification of their tribes the Mongols took over new, completely culturally different territory every 20 years: 1204 unification of the tribes, 1220 to the Caspian Sea, 1240 to Hungary, Silesia and Asia Minor, 1260 Persia and 1280 China. They are said to have been in Georgia in 1221 and in Moscow in 1237. So it was only after that that Baghdad fell.

Remark 2021:
I wrote my book 2013 as if I were firmly convinced of the phantom time. In 2021 I would have worked more with "maybe". I make few suggestions of my own. I hope it is always clear if it is someone else's ideas and research or my own. I should have used footnotes in the first part as well.

3 contracts Verdun, Mersen & Ribemont

I would like to briefly refer to the three divisions of the kingdom of Louis the Pious, son of Charlemagne, among the heirs, which appear to be absolutely "theoretical".

In the first division, the so-called "bowling alley" from Genoa up to Friesland, part of Italy and thus border area between France and Germany, is absolute nonsense in terms of national policy.
Never in history has land been divided up like this, because the smallest child and the oldest old man can work out on the five fingers of one hand that this stretch of land is divided up between France and Germany "but so quickly", that everyone thinks normally Man gives this first of the three famous (fictional) contracts straight away.

The second treaty will then be neatly divided between France and Germany (as it was bound to happen).

But the third contract is a gag in itself: Now Germany is assigned exactly the bowling alley from the first contract. Firstly, where is the protest from the French, and secondly: The third treaty would only be logical if the first two treaties didn't even exist. None of the three powers involved makes politics that idiotic. (The contract locations are probably unimportant.)

1001 nights, Arthurian legend, Charlemagne

Because the downfall of the Roman Empire is so inexplicable with the previous official historiography, 1000 books are being written to use emergency constructions to shed light on the darkness where nothing can be brought into it. If I accept the phantom time from 614 to 911 and paraphrase the story between Romans, Arabs, Persians and Germanic peoples correctly, then you can save yourself all this huge amount of patient paper.

The Romans get all kinds of reproaches made. But they fought back bravely. They did not (!) End up incompetent. That Aetius Flavius, the last Roman among the Huns, who did not even exist, should have grown up, is just ridiculous. Rather, he and the Visigoths stopped the Arabs in northern Spain.

The time lie brings a lot with it. It has to be filled with life. The Arabs and Persians invent the fairy tales from 1001 nights, the British King Arthur and the Franks (French and Germans) Charlemagne. Please take a look at practical politics. Geographically and temporally. It just couldn't have gone that way. The time of Charlemagne is composed like an opera.

King Arthur is a legendary figure who appears in many literary works of the European Middle Ages. From the late 9th century, British chronicles record the king's leading and successful participation in battles against the Angles, Jutes, and Saxons (Anglo-Saxons) who invaded there around 500 AD. Arthur is a legend, but it is not set in the European Phantom Age.

Christians as spies in Persia?

In the book "Das antike Persien" by Josef Wiesehöfer it is vividly described how the Christians in Persia (Iraq and Iran) could have acted on behalf of Constantine the Great and were thus exposed as Roman spies by the Persian government.

The reaction to not being absorbed by Christianity is all too human from a Persian point of view.

Instead of adopting the 300-year-old one-God belief, it was better to stick to the old traditions or to look for something else. An alternative would certainly be Islam in Arabia, which is only just being established and is therefore little known.

But when the storm breaks out on the Roman Empire, it is also on the rise among the Persians. There are first cautious attempts to get closer. But one does not want to make oneself religiously dependent on either the Romans or the Arabs, because that would inevitably also result in political dependence.

So Christianity emerged around 30 AD, Islam around 325 AD and the Islamic religion of the Shiites around 925, so everything at a distance of about 300 years.

Persia has had the following covenants since the death of Constantine the Great in 337 AD:

a) With the Arabs against East Stream (Byzantium) in the 4th century.
b) With the Turks against the Arabs around 540 AD
c) With the Byzantines against the Turks around 580 AD
   A century later, the Persian tribe of the Bujids then brought Islam into Persia, i.e. in the 10th century.

The number "21" magical?

There could be another reason why the beginning of spring falls on March 21st in Caesar's time. (Another reason than the advance of the beginning of spring from approx. 130 BC from March 1st to March 21st):

The number "21" is magical in that with a lunar calendar with 12 x 30 days = 360 days per lunar year every 4 years, the deviation from the solar calendar with 365.2422 days per tropical year is almost exactly 5 + 5 + 5 + 6 = 21 days, whereby the 6 days include the leap year every 4 years.

Therefore the question is whether Caesar switched from a lunar calendar to a solar calendar and chose March 21, June and December as a special day.

Otherwise nothing special can be determined on the 21st of the month (especially in Roman times). The Ides are in the middle of the month and the other special days of the Romans do not fall on a 21st or a 24th of a month.

You can turn and turn as you like with the assertion of the time counterfeiters that the beginning of spring was at the time of the Council of Nicaea in AD 325. fell on a March 21st:

When March 21st around AD 325 then, in Caesar's time, March 24th must have been the beginning of spring. The earth does not make a "jerk".
At most a false March 21st was celebrated in Caesar's time, which astronomically was March 24th. But who now thinks the Romans are so stupid?

Ancient astronomer incapable AND brilliant?

In the book "The sun" by Richard Cohen from the year 2012 among other things also the research results of antique astronomers are represented.

One does not get rid of the suspicion that here partly wrongly through the Middle Ages was handed down into the modern times, because on the one hand mathematical astronomical genius is paired with absolutely stupid ideas as only an early medieval monk without world experience can give from himself.

We have here e.g. Thales of Milet:
He is said to have known around 540 BC already quite exactly the diameter of the sun in relation to the diameter of the earth's orbit around the sun calculated, namely on 1 / 720ths. This is the ingenious side of him.
At the same time, according to Diogenes of Sinope, he is said to have imagined the Earth as floating on water like a cork. Moreover, the sun would be illuminated by the fire of the earth and the sun would circle around the earth.
I think, who can carry out so ingenious calculations, he must have been clearly aware of the nature and the relation to each other of sun and earth.
Probably already Thales has seen the sun in the center, as it was also seen by some astronomers among the Greeks of the antiquity. What is this nonsense with the "cork"?

The earth is - against better knowledge of the church - then also still a disk (for all the badly educated ones of the early Middle Ages or also for better educated ones), in order to make the traces of the time falsification as far as possible unrecognizable. There a smorgasbord of astronomical untruths is set up and the antique astronomers are handed down wrongly and represented for partly stupid, in order to save the Christianity before the Islam.

One gives always only small with obvious misconduct. So then the earth was no more a disk sometime, it is said suddenly even, the church would never have asserted this, and sometime the sun stands in the center of our planetary system and not the earth, because astronomers of the Renaissance and the Baroque deliver here clear proofs obvious for everybody.

A century later, a certain Oinopides of Chios, around 460 BC. Chr. the ecliptic, thus the inclination of the earth axis of the equator to the orbital plane of the earth around the sun, on 23 degrees and 45 minutes to calculate, which comes amazingly close to the actual inclination of 23 degrees and 27 minutes.

I ask myself here in all seriousness how one can calculate such beautifully exact geometry if one is not conscious about it, how the celestial bodies stand to each other and how they are built.

The parts that make these astronomers seem immature, like the floating cork, have sprung from some monk's brain or a higher echelon of the church or a government official of the Byzantine state who couldn't think of anything better.
The question is whether the figure of Claudius Ptolemy is not simply invented to let him hand down the ancient astronomers as it was convenient for the early medieval time fakers in Byzantium and Rome. It is well known that almost all writings of Hipparchus of Nicaea disappeared and everything was handed down only by the Egyptian astronomer Ptolemy.

Phantom time 1914: thought experiment

What would it look like in our time (around the year 2000 AD) if someone - in order to gain his position - inserts a period of 300 years into actual history as fictitious and falsifies history in his own way?

Let us assume that Germany and Austria had the need and the power to fictitiously push in 297 years after 1914 and to make up for the bitter defeats of two world wars.

The trigger for this action would be a sale of Central European culture to e.g. the increasingly powerful Chinese. The East Asians face the alternative of admiring the successes of the Russians in Central Europe or of being inspired by the German spirit.

The situation is like around AD 600. (= 900 AD) for Christianity around 2200 AD hopeless for Germans and Austrians. The two states are about to dissolve and are to be connected to the neighboring countries. Only the Chinese can still help. To do this, you falsify history and absolutely want her as a partner.

So we have the same distance between Constantine's death in AD 337. and the beginning of the 1st World War in 1914. Because 614 minus 337 results in 277 years and 1914 plus 277 results in the year 2191 (i.e. around 2200 AD).

If you add exactly 297 years to 1914, you get the "schnapps number" 2211!

In the year 2211, however, the Russians are so far that they have brought almost all of Central Europe under their control and are considering whether they should teach the Chinese their culture. The Germans would of course prefer the Chinese to embrace their Central European culture despite the adverse situation.

It would be as if the Vikings and Russians were considering whether they want to adopt the Byzantine-Roman culture and thus defend Christianity or make the Arab-Persian culture and thus Islam number 1 worldwide.

Now it is time to distribute the roles like in a play on the theater stage before we continue:

Germany plays Rome (the original country)
Austria plays Byzantium (the new, more powerful)
Russia plays Arabia (attacks Central Europe)
Chinese play the Vikings (attack everything)
The USA play the Germanic tribes (take over Central Europe)

The idea of the time forgers is that Germany and Austria will only be attacked from the west in 1914 and not from the east. Analogously, the Roman Empire is only oppressed by the Germanic peoples and only 300 years later by the Arabs. Similarly, the attack by the Russians did not take place in 1914, but only in 2211.

To this end, one must also claim that the earth is flat and the sun orbits the earth, although the forgers know better, in order to make it more difficult for future generations to verify the time forgery. In addition, one obtains severe penalties against doubters of the time lie. They are meticulously watched that they are burned as heretics. So in the Middle Ages, from around 2200.
But certainly with different terms and different methods.

The attack on the Austrian heir to the throne Franz Ferdinand by the Serbs did not have its time in June 1914, but only in June 2211. Islam is not analogous to AD 325. as a reaction to the Council of Nicaea, but without any logic and without any historical connection, apparently not until AD 622. founded in the middle of the phantom time.

Germany is more and more infiltrated by the western, more precisely, Anglo-Saxon culture of the USA, analogous to the Germanic military leaders in Roman service from the 4th century AD. Note also that (like the Swiss Guards in the Vatican) among the richest Roman families at times of Augustus and then bodyguards Teutons.

After Germany has apparently been massively weakened by national bankruptcy and absolutely incompetent, mentally ill politicians, as well as by US culture, the East then falls over East Germany and separates the areas east of the Oder-Neisse, namely (1945 plus 297 equal) 2242 AD, and not as actually happened in 1945 AD.

The Central Powers Germany and Austria do not want to give themselves the nakedness of having been defeated by the people from the East; above all, the legacy of Wilhelm II and Franz Joseph is to be greatly embellished. It looks as if only a few areas in the west, such as Alsace, have been lost analogously to Rome, Armenia to Persia.

Now the USA conquered Poland "behind" Germany in the first half of the 22nd century, analogous to the Visigoths who occupied Spain, which of course did not take place either.

The Germans apparently recaptured Poland from the United States in the middle of the 22nd century, just as Byzantium is said to be able to call parts of Spain and Tunisia its own for some time, but neither of which happened.
However, these fairy tales contribute to the fact that on the one hand the Chinese get great respect for the German culture, on the other hand the Vikings for the Byzantine culture.

126

Now the Russians are conquering Poland from the Germans in 2241 (actually 1944). Analogous to the Arabs, who took Tunisia from the Romans in 698 (actually 401). But not only Poland, but also East Germany 2242 (actually 1945).

The Germans can claim to have won a victory against the US when it came to the spoils of Poland (in the middle of the phantom period 1914-2211).

In order to get to Germany, the nations from the east must first conquer Austrian territories (as of 1914). Vienna (analogous to Byzantium) itself does not fall, Berlin (= Rome) is conquered by the USA (= Teutons) and not by the Russians (= Arabs). In retrospect, history is faked here. Because as we know, it was not the USA but the Russians who conquered Berlin. However, given the well-known power of the USA, it is easy to convince people that the North Americans did take Berlin in 1945.

The German spirit remains (analogous to the Christian faith), supported by the USA (analogous to the Germanic peoples).

The Chinese (analogous to the Vikings) should be inspired by the German spirit and not by the Russian spirit. In order to blind the Chinese, the Germans persuade the USA to do phantom time between 1914 and 2211 (analogous to 614 to 911). The USA is allowed to create a real super human for their nation: "Superman". Analogous to how the Teutons created a Charlemagne.

Some characters are still missing from the play:

Scandinavia plays Persia
fictional aquads play fictional Huns

It is now pretended that the Scandinavians (analogous to ancient Persians) are not being harassed by the Russians, but by the fictional Aquads (analogous to the fictional Huns) in order to push the successes of the Russians (analogous to the ancient Arabs) into the future.

Likewise, the fictional Aquades harass the USA (= Germanic peoples) and drive them towards the Central Powers Germany and Austria. This means that the USA had little ambition to invade there, but are urged to do so by the Aquades (analogous to the Teutons, who were hardly interested in invading Rome, but were urged to do so by the fictional Huns.)

Now the Russians do not come in 1914 or 1945, but approx. 300 years later and at the same time attack a) a large part of the areas of the Central Powers Germany and Austria and b) also all of Scandinavia (analogous to ancient Persia). The Austrians (analogous to Byzantium) have regained the territories in Central Europe that the Russians (analogous to Arabs) had apparently conquered in 2242 from the USA (analogous to vandals in Tunisia).

The Scandinavians (= ancient Persians) are in fact making their own direction of Russian governance in order not to get anything from the Russian mentality. And only very late. They don't want to have anything to do with the German mentality. In their eyes, it is enough if the USA has already adopted this style a little. The Chinese, however, are now finally on the German and not on the Russian side because of the phantom time.

This introduction of the phantom time from 1914 to 2211 is just a thought experiment.
Because then 1914 = 2211, like 614 = 911.

Fall of the Mayas in Mexico around 1000

Thor Heyerdhal had shown several times between 1947 and the 1970s that in antiquity the Indians rowed to Africa and Europe and, conversely, the inhabitants of the Mediterranean Sea (well before the Columbus year 1492) could have sailed to Central and South America with fairly simple ships and even rafts.

One has to be very surprised when two years after the discovery of the New World in 1492, i.e. 1494, the high authority of the Vatican contractually divides the globe according to degrees of longitude between Spain and Portugal. This division can still be seen today in Brazil and the Spanish-speaking part of Central and South America.

How beautifully can the world be estimated or even calculated so precisely as early as 1494, if people of the Middle Ages are said to have had no idea of the geometry of the earth and its size? It must have known about America before, centuries before.

The pyramids at the Majas in Mexico and the pyramids in Egypt refer to old relationships across the Atlantic. Admittedly, they were probably minimal, otherwise there might have been horses and bicycles in the new world and tomatoes and corn in the old world in ancient times.

But the author is a bit speculative when he claims that the decline of the high civilization of the Mayas around 1000 AD had something to do with the fact that Byzantines and Teutons sailed to the Caribbean to arrive at the time of the Ottonians and Pope New Year's Eve II To cause a bloodbath among the Mayans, because otherwise the caste educated there would have passed on the time lie from 614 to 911 AD to posterity.

Such a massacre would make the numerous attempts to explain how the high civilization of the Mayans might have perished, superfluous, as well as the countless attempts to explain the fall of Rome.

After all, the Majas knew about the rotation of the earth around the sun and were otherwise extremely well versed in astronomical time and space. Some ancient astronomers (or all of them?) Also knew that the earth revolves around the sun. What tricks Byzantium and Rome around here to preserve the honor of Christianity over Islam and the honor of the family of Constantine the Great?

Because a slaughter is being addressed here in order to enforce a time lie or to bring about the transition from antiquity to the Middle Ages on all levels: Something like the one suspected among the Mayans could well have taken place in Europe.

We know of murders of abbots in the 10th century, such as the famous abbot Hatto von Vich near Barcelona. He was one of the educators of Pope Silvester II, who in turn comes from the poorest of backgrounds as a tanner of Aurillac (Auvergne). 970 AD Hatto von Vich (related to the Hattons in Germany?) Is murdered in Rome. Perhaps he had protested strongly against the lie of time that Silvester II sold to the Germanic peoples and finally solidified it, in the sense of the Byzantines.

If the Mayas were already so raging, what did they do with the Persians so that these people no longer have the opportunity to prove the invented years between 614 and 911 today? The Persians cannot tell their own story in these 297 years, so they try to fill in the gaps with Christian chronicles that have been manipulated.

We know of innumerable scrolls of the Majas, which were destroyed at the time of the Spanish conquest of Central America. Only 4 roles survived this destruction of cultural property. The argument to speak with the presumption of "paganism" cannot be entirely accepted here. The "pagan" antiquity has been passed down in all its breadth. There is suspicion that evidence was destroyed.

Are volcanoes and supernova a trump card?

Serious lists of supernovae only start with that supernova in the year 1006 AD in the constellation Wolf. The older ones are actually only passed down by the Chinese. The Roman and Greek sources have probably "accidentally" disappeared during the transition into the Middle Ages. You have to be grateful that a figure like Cicero or other personalities of ancient times were handed down to the Middle Ages at all, since they were all attached to the polygod beliefs.

Dr. Illig complains that today's astronomers are not on his side and want to use supernovae (guest stars) to prove that the time between 614 and 911 actually existed. In his opinion, these astronomers would use the forged documents as evidence. A false tradition is conclusive in itself. You can no longer prove the opposite. To do this one would have to ask the people living at the time.

Wikipedia pages indicate that before 1006 the supernovae were only passed down by the Chinese. A bit strange. What about the classical Greek astronomers? There wasn't a supernova back then. And in the time of the Romans nobody was interested in it anymore?

During the volcanic eruptions that color the skies red and darken worldwide (at least for a year), only one is noticed. That of Mount Tauro on New Zealand either around 180 or 233 AD. There is another tolerance of 13 years in there. It was listed by the Chinese and the Romans. Not the eruption itself, but the red-discolored sky. A senior clergyman who held the original Roman document can destroy the original and put his own date on it.

If, for example, one takes the year 187 AD, then for synchronization with the Chinese, because there are no 297 supplemented years, it would actually have been the year 111 BC.

Second part – from my book 2019

Does Hatto window show 614 = 911 AD?

Hatto I. (+913), Chancellor & Archbishop, Hatto window

The so-called Hatto window (Hatto-Fenster) [1], an upright rectangular limestone block is exhibited today in the medieval section of the Cathedral and Diocesan Museum (inventory no. PS 00114) in Mainz/Germany. In 1861 it was discovered by Prelate Friedrich Schneider in the east wall of a vaulted cellar of the house "Zum Eckrädel", today Weintorstrasse 11, which was destroyed in the Second World War. This stone frame may have belonged to the former St. Mauritius Church, which was built in the late 9th century and was located here until 1814. The dimensions of the frame are: height 126.6; Width 75.5; Letters 2.5 (A), 5 (B), 2 (C) cm.

(A) A legend runs around the arched opening:
LVX ET SAL HATTHO S[ACRA]NS DIVI[NI]QVE SACERDO[S]
[H]OC TEMPLVM [STR]VXIT PICTVRA COMPSIT ET AVRO +

(B) It says on the upper frame strip:
DEXTERA [2] // D[OMI]NI F[ECIT] V[IRTVTEM]

(C) In the upper outer corners of the cross, two half-length portraits appear, which are identified as Michael and Gabriel by the inscriptions below:

---

[1] Postcard of Bischöfliches Dom- und Diözesanmuseum Mainz, Title: Hattofenster 1861 found near St. Mauritius, Mainz around 900, Foto: Alberto Luisa, München, Brescia
[2] DEXTRA is in the frame, with three short lines going to the left at the "R"

MICH[AEL] & GABR[IEL]

The translation is:
(A) light and salt. Hatto, the consecrator / bishop and priest of the divine, built this church / temple, adorned it with painting and gold.
(B) The right hand of the Lord has done great things. [3]

There is no lack of Christian symbols, such as the small cross after the AVRO, the hand between DEXTERA and DNIFV and two ornate crosses on poles, which conveniently separate inscriptions and decorative strips from each other.
Is there a hidden reference to the family of Archbishop Hatto I and / or the Illig phantom time in the so-called Hatto window?

Search for 1st clue:

The question arises as to why the name "HATTHO" was spelled that way, with an "H" in front of the "O". Perhaps the "H" before the "A" should also be discussed. In front of it there is a "SAL" (salt). These letters - incorporated into "ATTO" - result in an ATTALOS. The two "H" should probably be deleted.

---

[3] quoted:
http://www.inschriften.net/mainz/inschrift/nr/dio001-sn1-0002.html - DEUTSCHE INSCHRIFTEN ONLINE, Inschriftenkatalog: Mainz, DIO 1: Mainz (2011), SN1, Nr. 2 Dom- und Diözesanmuseum um 900, in this u.a. Prof. Arens quoted (with illustration Hattofenster)

Search for 2nd clue:

Can something be read from "LUX ET SAL"? It is known that Hatto I. is a good friend [4] by Bishop Solomon III. of Constance, who was abbot of St. Gallen from 890 to 919. [5] The first abbot of St. Gallen was 612-640 Gallus. It is said to come from Ireland, but could also be from the southern Vosges. [6] If the 297 years between 614 and 911 did not exist, SALomo would be the first abbot of St. Gallen and Gallus fictitiously. Came Solomon from Luxeuil (Roman: LUXovium) [7] and not from the area north of Lake Constance? Gallus was a student of Columban who built the monastery at Luxeuil. [8] Does Hatto I come from Langres and not from a noble Swabian family?

Friedrich Schneider pointed to an inscription from around 900 that was once on the choir arch, i.e. in the altar area, of the monastery church in St. Gallen: TEMPLVM QVOD GALLO GOZPERTVS STRVXERAT ALMO / HOC ABBAS YMMO PICTVRIS COMPSIT ET AVRO (This church, which Gozbert dem St. Gall, Abbot Immo decorated it with pictures and gold).

The symbol of DEXTRA DEI, which originated in Lombardy Italy in the 8th century, was not found on stone monuments north of the Alps (Mainz only) in the early Middle Ages, as Schulze-Dörrlamm rightly stated, but it was adorned from the 10th century at the latest numerous godparents and can

---

4 Wikipedia (germ.) „Salomo III. von Konstanz" (called 29.9.2019)
5 Wikipedia (germ.) „Liste der Äbte des Klosters St. Gallen" (called 29.9.2019)
6 Wikipedia (germ.) „Gallus (Heiliger)" (called 29.9.2019)
7 Wikipedia (germ.) „Luxeuil-les-Bains – französische Gemeinde" (called 29.9.2019)
8 Wikipedia (germ.) „Gallus (Heiliger)" (called 29.9.2019)

also be found on the manipula of St. Ulrich von Augsburg from the 3rd quarter of the 10th century. [9]

Search for 3rd clue:
A "G" is written like a "C", so that if you swap the two "C" you could see "MICH-CABR":

I (MI / mihi), Gregors (G) heir (H = heres), was deprived of Roman citizenship (C = civitas romana; civium = citizen) (ABR).

"ABR" could be an abbreviation for: Abradere = abzwacken; abripere = to snatch, to rob; abrogare = deny; abrumpere = tear off, break away. Does the "G" stand for Gregorius Attalus von Langres (450-539 / 40)? "H" can be used for "heritage".

This Archbishop of Mainz, Hatto I, is attributed with the fact that he, as a leading clergyman, prevented a merger with the West Franconian Carolingian Empire by proposing Count Konrad from the Lahngau (from Weilburg an der Lahn) as the first German king (911-918). [10] If, according to the Munich art historian Dr. Heribert Illig on August 31, 614 AD the next day of September 9, 911 AD then this would be a separation from the Merovingian Chlothar II, son of Fredegunde. It could be assumed that in the Merovingian Empire between 550 and 600 AD. Roman citizenship was withdrawn from all residents.

---

[9] http://www.inschriften.net/mainz/inschrift/nr/dio001-sn1-0002.html
[10] Gerlich: Hatto I. in: Lexikon des Mittelalters, Band 4

Hatto, derived from Attoariorum, Langres?

Another connection between the Hattons and Burgundy arises from the county of Atuyer (French for: Attoarii) in Burgundy, which existed until the 10th century. The area got its name from the Frankish people of the Chattuarii, some of whom were probably settled there. The pagus Attoariorum, mentioned since 658, enclosed the southwest of Langres (and included Dijon until around 770).

The "Pagus" came first under the sovereignty of the first dukes of Burgundy, then under the sovereignty of the bishops of Langres and the counts of Burgundy. After the division into the counties of Fouvent and Beaumont-s.-Vingeanne in the 10th century, the name Atuyer disappears from tradition. [11]

The Chattuari are not to be confused with the Chatti in Northern Hesse. They settled on the Lower Rhine on the border between what is now Germany and the Netherlands. However, Strabo names them in a group with the Cherusci, the Chatti and the Gamabrivii.

Strabo or Strabon was an ancient Greek writer. He lived from about 63 BC to after 23 AD and came from Amaseia in Pontos.

Hatto Bonosus - the link between Attalids and Hattons?

Hatto Bonosus was abbot of Fulda from 842 to 856. Even as an abbot, he was only a deacon. He should not be confused with Archbishop Hatto I of Mainz, who was never abbot of Fulda. There should have been stays at the royal court in

---

[11] Lexikon des Mittelalters, S.1182 (darin Quellenangabe: M.Chaume, Origines du duché de Bourgogne, Géogr. Hist. III, 1931)

the years 844, 845 and 849. Hatto Bonosus died on April 12, 856. [12]

A whole series of questions arise:
Is he a relative or even the father of Bishop Hatto I of Mainz (+913)?
Should this person be regarded either (a) as fictional because they lived in Illig"s phantom period 614 to 911 or (b) classified as real and thus (exactly?) Dating back 297 years. The consideration is invalid if one (c) considers the time between 614 and 911 to be real.
In case (b), Hatto Bonosus would have become the leading man on behalf of the Church in Fulda in 545 and would have passed away in 559.
Abbot Hatto I. Bonosus (+ "856") could perhaps have been the one who built the modest buildings in Fulda in the 9th (6th?) Century (south side of today's Domplatz) using ancient Roman construction technology.
The rooms were possibly destroyed by the (Lower) Saxons in the year 556. At that time the wars of the Franks against the Saxons waged between 555 and 558, with the Saxons advancing to Cologne-Deutz. Maybe Fulda also got it. [13]
There would then be two destructions that are exactly 297 years apart: The second is in the 9th century, on the night of September 1, 853, when thieves stole part of the church's treasure. [14]

I am of the opinion that - taking into account the lack of time from 614 to 911 - it could have happened that way. But that's pure speculation:
After the temporary orphanage of the Christian place of work Fulda 556, Abbot Hadamar (+956) resumed the Christian

---

[12] Schmid: Die Klostergemeinschaft von Fulda im frühen Mittelalter, Band 1, S.186
[13] Chronik der Deutschen, S.113
[14] Leinweber: Die Fuldaer Äbte und Bischöfe, S.24

mission there in 927 and had the first large church built between 937 and 948.

Another question is whether Hatto Bonosus (in other sources also referred to as Count on the Middle Rhine) comes from Burgundy and was related to the politically (secular and ecclesiastical) influential Attalids there. In terms of age, he could well have been a grandson of Gregor (ius) Attalus, Bishop of Langres (near Dijon) and high official in Autun.

Attalids 5th / 6th centuries – in Langres

In this chapter the family table for Gregor von Tours is used, as it can be found in: Martin Heinzelmann, Gregor von Tours (538-594), Ten Books of History, Wiss. Buchgesellschaft Darmstadt, 1994 (people numbered).

Attalus: grandson of Gregor Attalus von Autun?

It would be attractive if Hatto Bonosus is identical to a person who is shown on the family tree of Bishop Gregor von Tours (* 538, +594) (No. 3), created by Martin Heinzelmann (Darmstadt; * 1942 in Mannheim) .

Only person no. 11 with the name Attalus (* approx. 516), one of the grandsons of Gregorius Attalus von Langres (no. 14) would offer himself here.

The two other grandchildren Silvester (No. 10) and Eufronius (No. 12) could be excluded if it is plausible that they died in 572 and around / after 573. Because Hatto Bonosus is said to have passed away in 856. It would be 559 with phantom time.

This Attalus (No. 11) is in my opinion around 535 AD was not rescued by a cook Leo who was held hostage near Trier, but perhaps received spiritual training from the famous Trier Bishop Niketius (term of office 526-566, previously head of a monastery in Limoges). Gregor von Langres (No. 14) can allegedly "pick up" his grandson again in Reims. [15] Not a word is lost in this tragedy over Bishop Nicetius. Such a self-confident man, who stubbornly defended ancient culture in the Trier area and was respected by the Germanic princes, could easily have been used as a mediator for Gregor von Langres (No. 14).

The late Roman poet Venantius Fortunatus reports on a huge bishopric of Nicetius on a hill in a loop of the Moselle near Trier. The center is said to have been surrounded by

---

[15] Klopp: Aus deutscher Sage und Geschichte, Band 2, S.39

30 towers and a curtain wall, with ancient buildings such as a Greek temple. Were these buildings in Trier an incentive to build something ancient Roman in Fulda in the 6th century?

Martin Heinzelmann writes about this Attalus:

"Nepus (nephew) of Gregory of Langres. With other senator's sons he was brought to the Trier area around 532 as part of an exchange of hostages between the kings Childebert I and Theudebert. There he fell into state serfdom when the war broke out again. Since he is referred to as puer (dt: boy) around 532, like Bishop Eufronius (No. 12) he was probably not a nephew, but rather a grandson of Gregory of Langre. [...] What is noticeable about this episode is Hist. III.15, the only source for his existence, that it was not his parents but only his grandfather who tried to free him from serfdom. Accordingly, the parents died early. [...] "

The sister Armentaria (No. 9) of Silvester (No. 10) and Attalus (No. 11) and possibly of Eufronius (No. 12) was the mother of Gregory of Tours (No. 3). [16]

Gregory of Langres - Link to Roman counter-emperor

Bishop Gregor von Langres, his previous name was Attalus von Autun, who last lived in the better protected city of Dijon, was related to the historian Gregor von Tours (in Heinzelmann's family tree, Gregor von Tours can be found under No. 3 as mentioned).

Heinzelmann writes about this (among many other details): "He was the "top man" for Gregor von Tours, that is, the leading figure of a generatio [...] to which the great-grandson consciously linked. [...]

The chronology of his career is based on the vita, according to which Gregor von Langres died at the age of 90 (539/540). Before that he had held the episcopate of Langres for 32 years [...] after having been comes from Autun for 40 years.

---

[16] Heinzelmann: Gregor von Tours (538-594) „Zehn Bücher Geschichte", S.15

This would have given him the comitatus in Autun in 466 or 467 at the age of 16/17, which is conceivable if he has inherited the office." [17]

In Pauly-Wissowa, the standard work for the description of ancient people, under the 20th "Attalos" is:
"An A. (Attalos), perhaps a grandson of the previous one, was soon after 470 Curator civitatis Aeduorum. Addressed to him Apollo. Sid. ep. (Letter from Appollinaris Sidonius) V 18. " [18]

The "previous one" is the 19th "Attalos", namely "Priscus Attalos".[19] This was the Roman counter-emperor at the beginning of the 5th century. This man had a son Ampelius. In my opinion he would then have to be the father or uncle of Gregor von Langres, if Pauly-Wissowa is right that Priscus Attalus (or Attalos) could be a grandfather.
With "Civitas Aeduorum" is meant Autun, which was called Augustodunum under Rome. It was the capital of the Haeduer. [20] A "curator" is a senior civil servant.

For the following two family trees also look at the source "Heinzelmann, Gregor von Tours" The members of the Attalus family are numbered there. Most interesting is the person No. 11., which could connect the 6th century with the 10th century.

---

[17] Heinzelmann: Gregor von Tours (538-594) „Zehn Bücher Geschichte", S.17f.
[18] Pauly-Wissowa, Keyword in the lexicon: „Attalos", S.2179
[19] Pauly-Wissowa, Keyword in the lexicon: „Attalos", S.2177ff.
[20] Paulys Realencyklopädie (1896), Band II,2, S.2368

Family tree Hattons in the early Middle Ages

Hatto Bonosus (identical with Attalus [No. 11]?)
*about 516 (813) as Attalus of Langres?
+856 (in Fulda or in Mainz?)
Count on the Middle Rhine, nobillisimus dux ac consul
Student of Niketius (Bishop of Trier 527-563/566)?
Abbot of Fulda 842-856 / Builder of the villa rustica in Fulda? 556
(853) destroyed by the Saxons?

Hatto I.
*about 550 (about 850)
+913 in Mainz
first (?) Archbishop of Mainz 594 (891) -913
Pallium 599 (896) by Pope Gregor the Gr. (like Bishop of Autun)
Regent for Ludwig, the child (last East Franconian Merovingian?)
Chancellor of King Konrad I (Count im Lahngau)

Hadamar
* around 600 (around 900) in Langres (?)
+956 in Cologne on King Otto the Great's court day
Abbot of Fulda 927-956
important advisor to Otto the Great (+973)
Pope visits 936, 943, 947 and 955
Obtaining the pallium 955 from the Pope for Cologne Bishop Brun

Hatto II. [according to Marianus Scottus: "Nephew of Hadamar"]
* before 930 (due to Hadamar accompanying him to Rome 936)
+970 in Mainz
Abbot of Fulda 956-968
Archbishop of Mainz 968-970
prepares the coronation of Otto the Great in Rome in 961 in 962
with Pope John XII. (Octavian) ahead

Hatto III.
* around 950/970
+997 in the Fulda monastery
Monk in Fulda 987-991
Abbot of Fulda 991-997
prepares Otto III's coronation as emperor in Rome in 994. with Pope
John XV. before (on behalf of grandmother Adelheid, widow of Otto
the Great)

Family tree of Attalus leads to Hattons?

P. Ampelius
Roman official from Antioch:
first Praeses Cappadociae and Magister Officiorum, then:
Proconsul Achaiae 359 AD,
Proconsul Africae 364 AD,
City prefect of Rome 370-372 AD.

Attalus Priscus
Magistrate in Rome 394 AD.
Envoy to the emperor in 398 AD. and 409 AD.
City prefect of Rome and Comes sacrarum largitionum 409 AD.
Conversion from the Greek belief to Arianism / Christianity
counter-emperor 409-410 / 414-415 n.Chr. with visigoths support.

Ampelius
In the Visigoth camp in 410 AD. in the south of France

Attalus of Autun = Gregor of Langres
* approx. 450 +539 or 540
466/467 comitatus in Autun, shortly after 470 Curator civitatis
Aeduorum
Bishop of Langres since 406 or 407, resident in Dijon
(According to Pauly-Wissowa, the man in Autun could be a
grandson of the Roman counter-emperor Attalus Priscus)

**Grandson Attalus
[No. 11]**

Hatto Bonosus (No. 11?)
+ 859
Identical to grandson Attalus?
(if the time 1.9.614 to 31.8.911
did not exist?)
Also related, if there is time, but a
difference of 300 years?

143

Hademar, Hatto 10th century – from Langres?

Hadamar and Hademar are said to be derived from Old High German, namely from the two words "hadu" (fight, quarrel) and "mar (i)" (famous, mar). So it is in countless books that explain first names. [21]

When describing the villages of Oberhadamar and Niederhadamar, the meaning "contested waterhole" is also attached. [22]

The origin and meaning of the name "Hatto" can be found: Old High German, short form of a name made up of "hadu" (fight, cf. nhd. Hadern) and another unknown component (such as Hadubrand, Hadbert, Hadwin). [23]

"Placed traces" are a fact, with or without 614 to 911

In my opinion, the first names or names "Hatto" and "Hadamar" in the early Middle Ages could not (only) have been borne by Germanic tribes, but (also) by Gallo-Romans. In order to keep up with the new zeitgeist from around 500 or 900 AD to correspond, giving up or discarding the ancient Roman name would be conceivable (or even a regulation of the mighty).

Several traces seem to have been deliberately laid in the 10th century - mainly from Fulda. (The question is incidentally, since when have the places Hadamar and Haddamar actually been named.).

---

[21] www.kirchenweb.at/vornamen/namenstage/vornamen08. htm (called 4.8.2019)

[22] Wikipedia (germ.) „Geschichte der Stadt Hadamar" (called 4.8.2019)

[23] Wikipedia (germ.) „Hatto (männlicher Vorname)" (called 4.8.2019)

I suspect that could be derived:

1) Hatto (also Atto, Azzo) from: Attoariorum (area around Langres)
2) Hademer (also Ademer etc.) from: Andemantunnum (Langres)

Then we have the Niederhadamar-Haddamar-Fulda-Langres trapeze. (See below)
In addition, we have very good relations with Rome and the very high positions in church positions in Fulda and Mainz in the 10th century.
How exactly the Hattons (or a part of them) could be related to the Attalids in Burgundy (if at all!) Can of course no longer be determined.

Even regardless of whether the time was from Sept. 1, 614 to Aug. 31, 911 or not, whether you are an opponent or supporter of Illig's phantom time theory, these traces are there. What I find most impressive is the trapeze in the landscape.
So also with the 9th, 8th and 7th centuries, the (obviously deliberately laid) traces point to an origin of the Hattons and the abbot Hadamar from the area around Langres in France. This is particularly true of the Abbot Hadamar.

It may be that I am wrong about this too.

In the daily newspaper "Bieler Tagblatt" (Switzerland) of Sept. 27, 2019, a grave relief from Pompeii is shown on page 11. Among other things, it says: "Marble, before 79 AD, from the Museo Archeologico Nazionale in Naples."
The color of the stone is light brown. On the edge strips on the left and right there are similar decorations as on the Hatto window, also on the left and right: There are ornaments from palmette tendrils on the Hatto window and possibly something similar on the grave relief from Pompeii. It also seems as if numerous people wander through the relief, as in the baseboard of the Hatto window. Only there are no crosses in Pompeii.

Attalids in antiquity, classical era

Attalus Priscus, Roman counter-emperor

Attalus Priscus was AD 409 and 414-415. Roman counter-emperor. By baptism before Sigesarius, bishop of the Visigoths, he converted from the ancient belief in many gods to Christianity. [24] His son Ampelius went to Gaul with the Visigoths.

Roman coin of Attalus Priscus
Silver coin with a portrait of the Roman emperor Attalus Priscus in:
Attalus Priscus Wiki (french, spanish),
https://commons.wikimedia.org/w/index.php?curid=384193 /
S.239

---

[24] Pauly-Wissowa, Keyword in the lexicon: „Attalos", S.2177

Other Attalids in antiquity, selection

After the fall of the empire of Pergamon in 133 BC. we have - in addition to about 15 other people listed in Pauly-Wissowa - the following Attalids:

• Around 90 BC. in Athens
• Teacher of Seneca (teacher of Emperor Nero)
• "Attalus of Pergamon", who dies as a Christian and a martyr in Lyon, under the rule of Marcus Aurelius.
• At about the same time an Attalos Paterklianos lives in Pergamon. During the excavations around 1900, his exceptionally large villa was found in the city of Pergamon. There is talk of big celebrations.
• Condemned at the time of Emperor Commodus (son of Marcus Aurelius).
• King of the Marcomanni, at the time of the Roman emperor Philipus Arabs.

Before the kings in Pergamon, it is worth mentioning an Attalus (general of Philip II of Macedonia), whose niece married Alexander's father in a second marriage.

Abbot Hadamar von Fulda (* around 900, +956)

The first extensively described person who made the name "Hadamar" known is the famous abbot of Fulda. Outside of the relatives of King Otto the Great, he was probably his most important advisor in the early days of his reign.

King Heinrich I. (+936)

From the year 927 we know him as abbot of the monastery in Fulda. The year 927 is interesting because from this year clergymen can be found for the first time at the court or in the chancellery of the German or rather East Franconian King Heinrich I. The number of certificates has also increased since then.[25]

The only meeting between Abbot Hadamar and King Heinrich (+936) is documented for the year 932.[26] At that time there was a synod in Erfurt. There, before the king, the abbot is said to have exchanged the royal estate in Abenheim in Wormsgau for property in Thuringia and Saxony.

King Otto I, the Great (+973)

The relationship between Abbot Hadamar and Heinrich's son Otto the Great (* 912, +973 in Memleben) is based on great state policy. After Heinrich died on July 2nd, 936, and Otto the Great was crowned his successor on August 8th, 936, Otto confirmed the privileges of the Fulda Monastery on October 14th of the same year and later gave "to his (ie Otto) and his father (ie Heinrichs) Seelenheil "allegedly gave Abbot Hadamar his property at Northeim in the Salzgau.[27]

In 939 Otto the Great made use of the abbot's services. A rebellion led by Otto's brother Heinrich and the dukes

---

[25] Nitschke: Die Ottonen, ein Herrscherhaus aus Sachsen, S.331

[26] Leinweber: Die Fuldaer Äbte und Bischöfe, S.30ff.

[27] Leinweber: Die Fuldaer Äbte und Bischöfe, S.30ff.

Eberhard of Franconia and Giselbert of Lorraine beats Otto down near Andernach on October 2nd. While Eberhard, a brother of the first East Franconian king Konrad I, is being killed by relatives, Giselbert drowns in the Rhine, at least according to the story.

Friedrich, Bishop of Mainz since 937, was captured by Otto because he had supported the uprising and placed under house arrest for a year, first in Fulda, then on the Hammelburg, each time under the supervision of Abbot Hadamar von Fulda. Abbot Hadamar initially held Bishop Friedrich in honorable custody. He later tightened it after uncovering a prohibited correspondence. Friedrich is said to have never forgotten the treatment he received from the abbot. After the release from prison, according to Widukind, severe persecution within the East Franconian church should have started by the bishops: Anyone who did not lead an impeccable way of life in the monastery was driven out of it. Behind all this stood Bishop Friedrich von Mainz (+954), who only pursued this reform in order to "injure" Abbot Hadamar von Fulda.[28] I think he, the abbot, could certainly have been given a lot of credit because he was quite unconventional. The friendship with Otto the Great probably saved him from worse.

Hadamar's nephew Hatto II (+970) and 1st trip to Rome 936

Abbot Hadamar traveled to Rome for the first time in the spring of 936, when the government of King Henry I was in his last breath, probably via the Reichenau Monastery on Lake Constance. On May 13th of the same year Pope Leo confirmed the privileges of the Fulda Monastery. With him and only on this first of four trips to Rome he had his nephew Hatto II, the son of Hadamar's sister, who was to

---

[28] Fried: Das Reich der Ottonen, S.502

follow him as abbot in Fulda and even became archbishop of Mainz from 968 to 970.[29]

Here, at least once, a relationship with the "Hattons" can be proven from a "Hadamar".

Another 3 trips to Rome, Synod in Ingelheim, Fulda

During his second trip to Rome at the end of March 943, the abbot received confirmation of the privileges from Pope Marinus II. However, this trip does not only seem to have served the interests of the monastery, because immediately after returning, Hadamar went to Balgstädt to the king to report on an unspecified assignment and to deliver letters from the Pope. Otto also confirmed older rights of the monastery in Fulda to the abbot at the time.

In the autumn of 947 Hadamar traveled a third time to Rome, again on behalf of the king. It is said to have been about the establishment of new missionary dioceses. On January 2nd, 948, the abbot again received confirmation of the privileges of his monastery from Pope Agapet II. Without this being handed down, it can be strongly assumed that Hadamar negotiated with Agapet about papal mediation in French and West Frankish affairs. The result of this was the synod in Ingelheim near Mainz in 948.[30]

The powerful Duke Hugo von Franzien, ancestor of the Capetians, had deposed the reigning King Ludwig IV in 945. Thereupon Otto I moved to France to support his brother-in-law and was able to take Reims. In June 948, after Ludwig IV's complaint, Hugo was excommunicated in front

---

[29] Schmid: Die Klostergemeinschaft von Fulda im frühen Mittelalter, Band 1, S.191. That it is supposed to be the son of his sister is passed down to us from the Marianus Scottus (+1086) in the 11th century. The historian was from 1058 to 1069 Rekluse near the Fulda Michaelskapelle - like the first cathedral - built in the 10th century.

[30] Lexikon des Mittelalters: Keyword „Hadamar, Abt"

of a papal legate in Ingelheim.[31] In addition, it is decided in Ingelheim to found new dioceses "in the north".

On November 1st, 1948, the papal legate Marinus von Bomarzo consecrated the monastery church in Fulda, which was (in my opinion only) built by this abbot. Today's cathedral has stood in the same place since the baroque era. Around 550 there was a "Villa Rustica". For more information, see "Hessen in the Early Middle Ages Archeology and Art", edited by Helmut Roth and Egon Wamers, published in 1984 by Jan Thorbecke Verlag (see also below).

Hungary 955, pallium for Cologne, death 956

Meanwhile new calamities were brewing over King Otto I. During the beginning of January 953 the king was accompanied [32] of Abbot Hadamar von Fulda and his brothers Brun and Heinrich via Frankfurt to Erstein, south of Strasbourg, rode to a meeting of the bishops and dukes of the Eastern Empire, forged Konrad the Red, since 944 Duke of Lorraine and great-grandfather of the first Salier on the German throne, a coup. The uprising was put down. Lorraine went to the Archbishop of Cologne, Brun, Otto's younger brother. On August 10th, 1995, Otto I finally drove the Hungarians out of the East Franconian Empire through a victory on the Lechfeld near Augsburg. Abbot Hadamar is said to have conveyed the news of the victory personally to Pope Agapet II on his fourth and last trip to Rome in the late summer of 955. In Rome he asked for the pallium for Bishop Brun of Cologne and brought it to him in the late autumn of 955. Because of the success of the negotiations with the Pope, he can inform King Otto I that dioceses can now be set up by the king as he wishes. Otto had the plan to move the seat of the Halberstadt diocese to Magdeburg and to raise Magdeburg to an independent archdiocese to which the

---

[31] Mann: Universalgeschichte in Stichworten, Band 5, S.637
[32] Wies: Otto der Große, Kämpfer und Beter, S.143

future mission dioceses in the east should be subordinate. In doing so, however, he encountered the interests of the then Bishop of Mainz, Wilhelm, a natural son of Otto the Great with a Slavic. Wilhelm (954-968 Archbishop), just appointed vicar for "Gaul and Germania" by the Pope [33], did not want to lose either his suffragan diocese of Halberstadt or the opportunities for expansion for his church province in the east. He refused to approve the planned project. Abbot Hadamar (as the mediator of the agreement reached behind Wilhelm's back) felt Wilhelm's whole anger. In a letter to the Pope, he described the abbot as a false prophet, who went to Rome as a wolf in sheep's clothing, hung himself with gold and pearls and publicly boasted that he could have bought as many pallia in Rome for 100 pounds of money as he did he would have wanted.[34]

Stays at the royal court are documented for the year 932 with Heinrich I and for the years 936, 943, 948, 951 and 953 with Otto I (the great). In 948 Otto I probably visited Fulda on the occasion of the consecration of the church by Marinus. [35]

On May 25, 1995, Abbot Hadamar succumbed to an epidemic that had been rampant in the empire since spring. When King Otto the Great called for a court day in Cologne, the Archbishop Rotbert von Trier and the Fulda Abbot Hadamar suddenly differed. At least that's what Adalbert von Weißenburg reported.[36]

He was buried in the western choir of the Fulda monastery church. From there, however, his body was transferred in 1728 to the Marienkapelle of the Fulda Cathedral, which served as a monk's culture in the 18th century.

---

[33] Beumann: Die Ottonen, S.82

[34] Leinweber: Die Fuldaer Äbte und Bischöfe, S.30ff.

[35] Schmid: Die Klostergemeinschaft von Fulda im frühen Mittelalter, Band 1, S.190

[36] Hiller: Otto der Große und seine Zeit, S.181

Above the left entrance in the eastern part of the monastery church, which served as the main entrance, there was an inscription requesting those entering to bow their knees before Christ and pray for Abbot Hadamar.

In addition to the nickname "The Pious", which he received in his monastery after his death, a ten-verse poem preserved him an honorable memory. He himself had looked after his memory through a rich commemorative foundation. In addition to the usual provision of bread and wine, this included a donation of the poor. Abbot Hadamar was also remembered by a precious bowl he had acquired for the monastery church, which was stolen from the monastery in 1146 along with other jewels. [37]

With Abbot Hadamar begins the predominantly political activity of the Abbots of Fulda and the decline of monastic life, it is said in his literature. [38]

[37] Leinweber: Die Fuldaer Äbte und Bischöfe, S.30ff.
[38] Sturm: Die Bau- und Kunstdenkmale der Stadt Fulda, S.28

Do parallel air lines show 614 = 911 AD?

Train of thought

I had always wondered why two communities in the German state of Hesse bear the name of the famous Abbot Hadamar von Fulda. All the more so because the locations - apparently arbitrarily positioned - were created near Limburg an der Lahn (town of Hadamar) and near Kassel and Fritzlar (village of Haddamar). At first you don't have much to do with Fulda. If I first look at the angle to the latitude between Hadamar and Haddamar, I come to about 44 degrees. I noticed that on May 2, 2019.

Trapezoid 1: Fulda – Langres & Hadamar – Haddamar

Then on Saturday, May 4th, 2019 in Biel (CH) I bought a map of southern Germany on which even the village of Haddamar near Kassel was drawn.

1. I connected Haddamar near Kassel and Hadamar near Limburg a.d. Lahn with a straight line.
2. parallel to this line I drew a 2nd line from Fulda to the southwest. Then one reaches at some point Langres (north of Dijon, south of Toul resp. Nancy) in France.

For the second step, I took another map of France.

That I reached Langres with these two parallel air lines, I found already amazing! But how exactly is that correct? Drawing is one thing, but calculating exactly is another.

If someone has put here in the early Middle Ages with intention the two places Hadamar and Haddamar in such a way, then still 2 further "degrees of freedom" are open:

154

- Equal distance of the 2 places to the line Fulda-Langres still variable.
- Positions of the places on line Hadamar-Haddamar still variable.

The first degree of freedom is destroyed by the parallelism to Langres-Fulda. The next degree of freedom will be eliminated by a well meaningful distance to this line. The third and last degree of freedom of the positions of Hadamar and Haddamar will be dissolved by a bearing on Rome. More about this further below.

It will turn out further below mathematically that Niederhadamar fits better than Hadamar, which is situated just north of it.
The distance between Fulda (cathedral or cathedral square, where the Villa Rustica stood) and Haddamar (thoroughfare on the northern edge) near Fritzlar is 49.5 Roman miles.

That is 33.0 Roman leagues! This interesting distance is calculated below using the coordinates from Google Maps.

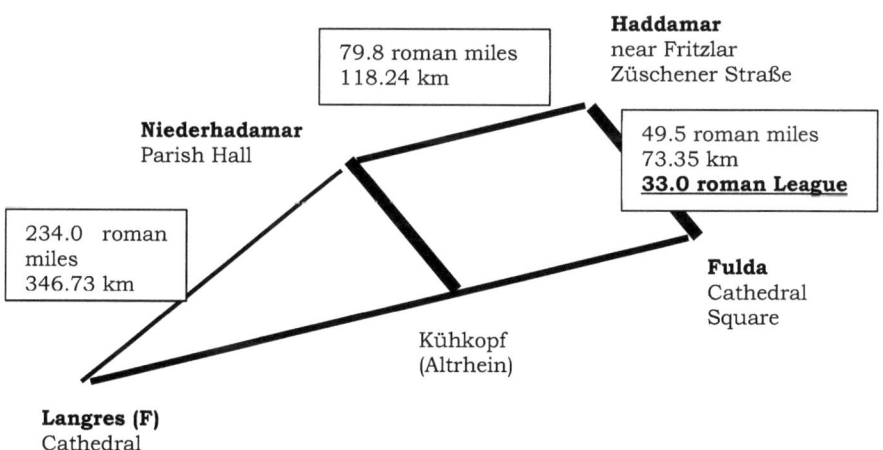

79.8 roman miles
118.24 km

Haddamar
near Fritzlar
Züschener Straße

Niederhadamar
Parish Hall

49.5 roman miles
73.35 km
33.0 roman League

234.0 roman miles
346.73 km

Fulda
Cathedral
Square

Kühkopf
(Altrhein)

Langres (F)
Cathedral

Coordinates Langres and Fulda - air line 1

In the times of Abbot Hadamar, the city of Langres already had an ancient past behind it. It was called Andematunnum. The old town is surrounded by a wall and is situated on a hill.
The city is far from industrial centers and today has as many inhabitants as at the end of the 18th century.
If you take the shortest route from Delémont in Switzerland to Paris, you will pass through this city. Likewise, if you take the highway from Saarbrücken to Dijon and on to Marseille, you will pass through this city.
Just east of the city there is a watershed. South of it the waters flow into the Mediterranean, north of it to the north.

In the center of the (old) city is the following prominent structure:

Langres Cathedral: 47.8646° North, 5.3348° East.

In Fulda, today's Domplatz (cathedral square) catches the eye (east of the cathedral). There, during excavations around 1900, a Villa Rustica from the 6th century was found, built according to ancient models. The grave of an "Otto" (from the 10th century) is also located there.

Villa Rustica, Fulda: approx. 50.5538° North, 9.6727° East (northern end of the path "Domplatz" according to Google Maps, southeast of the cathedral)

Coordinates Niederhadamar and Haddamar – air line 2

The castle of the Counts of Nassau (built from about 1325) and the stone bridge north of it (built in 1571, oldest parts from the 12th century) are prominent landmarks in Hadamar near Limburg a.d. Lahn. However, they did not exist at the time of Abbot Hadamar.

Hadamar (also "Mönchhadamar" or "Oberhadamar") was founded around 1190 by the Cistercian monastery of Eberbach in the Rheingau. On the area of the castle there was a farm of the monastery afterwards.

Hadamar Castle: 50.4475° North, 8.0453° East
Stone bridge: 50.4487° North, 8.0446° East

Niederhadamar, located south of (Upper) Hadamar, is smaller but has a longer history. It has probably been settled since 1000 BC. The center of the village is located at the old community center. This coordinate fits well for the considerations. It should also be mentioned the Wendelinus bridge.

Old parish hall: 50.4355° North, 8.0346° East
Wendelinus bridge: 50.4307° North, 8.0383° East

Celtic sites on the lower Elz (flows into the Lahn near Limburg) existed at Dornburg (north of the municipality of Hadamar) and at Steinbach. The area was just in the free Germania in the Roman times around 100 to around 250 AD. The Roman Limes runs through further west near Bad Ems.
The village of Haddamar near Fritzlar in northern Hesse was first mentioned in a document in 1209. The document can be found in the collegiate archives of Fritzlar. The village belonged to the landgraviate of Hesse. From 1386 to 1485 the lords of Hertingshausen are attested as owners. In 1427 the village was burned down by Mainzian troops under Gottfried von Leiningen.

In the case of this village it is not clear which position is important for this study of the Hadamar-Haddamar and Fulda-Langres axes. The question is: which prominent points in or near the village already existed in the 10th century?

157

Züschener Street: 51.1610° North, 9.2646° East
Village center: approx. 51.1598° North, 9.2658° East

Marked could be this thoroughfare at the northern edge of the village, because it is exactly 33.0 roman leugen to the cathedral square in Fulda. (see also below)

Forkenburg near Haddamar and others

Near Haddamar near Fritzlar or Kassel there are very old landmarks, some of which were already known in the 10th century. Among them, the Forkenburg is the hottest landmark, because it is located only 1 km from Haddamar.

The Forkenburg is a former flying or rampart castle in the district of Wehren. Other names are "Fackenburg" and "Vockenburg". It was built at the latest in the 10th century. It is a lowland castle, and only the rampart is still recognizable. It lies about 1 km WSW of Wehren and about 1 km NE of Haddamar on a low, spur-like promontory north above the meadow bottom of the small Klingelborn stream coming from Haddamar, which flows into the Eder tributary Ems near Wehren.

Forkenburg: 51.1653° North, 9.2812° East

The Wotanstein in Maden near Gudensberg has existed since the 3rd century BC The Wotanstein, made of quartzite, is almost 2 m high, 1.2 m wide and 0.55 m thick. A use as a place of assembly is possible.

Wotanstein: 51.1634° North, 9.3704° East

The stone chamber grave near Züschen would have to be omitted, because it was discovered only in 1894. The origin

158

is about 3500 to 2800 BC But maybe together with the Forkenburg it makes the Züschen road in Haddamar plausible for the 10th century.

Stone chamber grave near Züschen:
51.1739° North, 9.2405° East

Niedenstein near Haddamar

In my estimates of the parallelism of the air lines leading to Langres and Rome, the air lines seem to meet at Niedenstein (north of Haddamar). However, a more precise calculation is needed for clarification. Nevertheless, some coordinates of the village:

North part (main street) 51.2361° North; 9.3102° East.
Southern part ("Am Ziegenberg"): 51.2300° N; 9.3138° E
South part ("Friedensstraße") 51.2301° N; 9.3162° E

Trapezoid 1: Calculation of the parallelism (air lines 1 & 2)

On maps, the Fulda-Langres air route looks almost parallel to the Niederhadamar-Haddamar air route. How does it look mathematically?

The coordinates of the places are:

P	X = East	Y = North	Village/Town
1	5.3348°	47.8646°	Langres, Cathedral
2	9.6727°	50.5538°	Fulda, Domplatz
3	8.0346°	50.4355°	Niederhadamar
3a	8.0453°	50.4475°	(Ober-) Hadamar
4	9.2649°	51.1607°	Haddamar
4a	9.3138°	51.2300°	Niedenstein, Ziegenberg

Here are also indicated other places for testing, which are located nearby.

As the crow flies 1, coordinates of locations 1 and 2:

$$P_1 = \begin{pmatrix} x_1 \\ y_1 \end{pmatrix} \qquad P_2 = \begin{pmatrix} x_2 \\ y_2 \end{pmatrix}$$

As the crow flies 2, coordinates of locations 3 and 4:

$$P_3 = \begin{pmatrix} x_3 \\ y_3 \end{pmatrix} \qquad P_4 = \begin{pmatrix} x_4 \\ y_4 \end{pmatrix}$$

Ratios of coordinates are:

$$Ratio\ (air\ line\ 1) = \frac{\Delta\ Latitude}{\Delta\ Longitude} = \frac{(y_1 - y_2)}{(x_1 - x_2)}$$

$$Ratio\ (air\ line\ 2) = \frac{\Delta\ Latitude}{\Delta\ Longitude} = \frac{(y_3 - y_4)}{(x_3 - x_4)}$$

Then it results (once written down in detail):

(Langres Dom North – Fulda Dom North) / (Langres Dom East – Fulda Dom East)
(47.8646° - 50.5538°) / (5.3348° - 9.6727°) = -2.6892° / -4.3379° = **0.6199 ≈ 0.62**

Δ latitude / Δ longitude for this and other air lines (LL):

LL	Village/Town 1	Village/Town 2	Δ Lati /Δ Long
1	Langres	Fulda	0.6199 ≈ 0.62
2	Niederhadamar	Haddamar	0.5894 ≈ 0.59
2'	Oberhadamar	Haddamar	0.5847 ≈ 0.58
2''	Niederhadamar	Niedenstein, Zieg.	0.6205 ≈ 0.62
2'''	Niederhadamar	Forkenburg	0.5854 ≈ 0.59

Conclusion:
- Niederhadamar fits better than Oberhadamar
- Quotient fits better at point north of Haddamar: Niedenstein
- Parallelism is still very good at Haddamar
- Forkenburg and Haddamar near Fritzlar give almost the same result

The quotient of the two values is equal to one and the difference of the two values is zero. So the lines are parallel.

$\frac{(y_3-y_{4a})}{(x_3-x_{4a})} / \frac{(y_1-y_2)}{(x_1-x_2)}$ = 0.62 / 0.62 = 1

$$\frac{(y_3-y_{4a})}{(x_3-x_{4a})} - \frac{(y_1-y_2)}{(x_1-x_2)} = 0.62 - 0.62 = 0$$

Result:
Here Niedenstein fits very well to the parallelism, because the other air line then runs exactly towards the cathedral in Langres.

The air line Niederhadamar-Niedenstein runs further east through the Druseltal in Kassel. This remark only in the margin.

=> Trapezoid 1 parallel Δ 8.4 km NNO Haddamar

Exact parallelism of the two air lines – in the north Niederhadamar-Haddamar and in the south Langres-Fulda – seems to result if one pushes away from the village Haddamar near Fritzlar the point 8.4 kilometers to the north-northeast. There lies the municipality of Niedenstein.

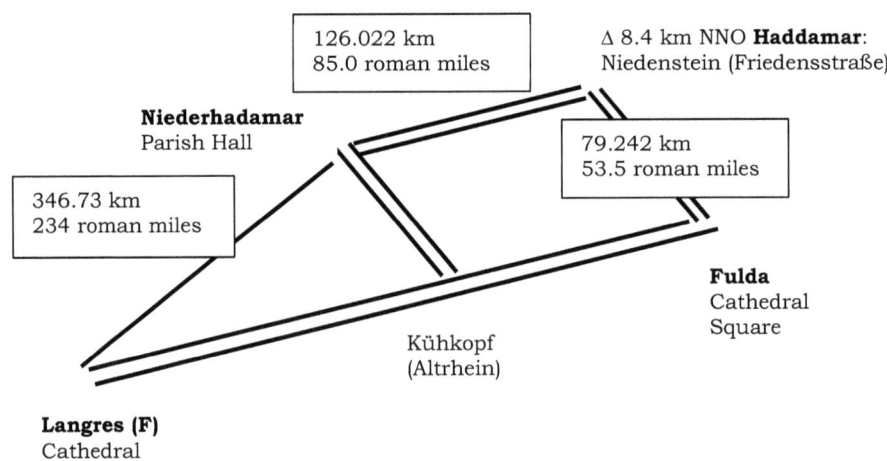

Parallelogram 1: Fulda (-Langres) to Altrheinaue Kühkopf

Here we have two unknowns in the formula, because the north coordinate depends on the east coordinate and vice versa. We dissolve the formula after the north coordinate and set several east coordinates as a test. Then we look whether both coordinates are still in the area of the floodplain of the Kühkopf.

Kühkopf North = (0.6199 * (Kühkopf East - Fulda East)) + Fulda North
= (0.6199 * (8.4263°- 9.6727°)) + 50.5538° = 49.781°

The position is between Gimbsheim and Biebesheim, on the south side of the floodplain.
Together with Niederhadamar-Haddamar (Niedenstein) the line Fulda-Altrheinaue (Kühkopf) forms a parallelogram. There on the Rheinaue there is a point where the distances of the two air lines are equal. There the trapezoid becomes a parallelogram.

Trapezoid 2 Rome – Niederhadamar & Fulda – Haddamar

Another question is whether the positions on the air line Haddamar-Hadamar could also mean something.

- One could also have placed Hadamar on the Rhine and
- Haddamar further to the east into Thuringia and
- still one would have had a parallel from Fulda to Langres.

Here an extension of the axis of Hadamar or Niederhadamer would have to be investigated. Where does this air line run parallel to the air line Fulda-Haddamar?
Answer: It reaches the Italian capital Rome. However, only if one (again) pushes the point in Haddamar near Fritzlar over 7 km to the east.

Coordinates in Rome - air line 4

Rome would have these buildings ready for parallel air lines "for religious reasons":

Lateran Palace: 41.8866° North, 12.5059° East
Church of St. Lawrence "outside the walls" 41.9026° North, 12.5208° East
Mausoleum of Constantia 41.9226° North, 12.5174° East.

As the crow flies no. 4 is the one from Niederhadamar to Rome.
As the crow flies, line No. 3 is from Fulda to Haddamar. All coordinates except that of Rome have been given above.
If you choose points further to the west of Rome, then the axis Fulda-Haddamar in the north also tilts further to the east, so away from Haddamar to the east. Therefore, only reference points in the east of Rome come into question.

The Lateran was since the time of Emperor Constantine the Great (+337) the official seat of the popes.[39] The Church of St. Lawrence Outside the Walls became the Patriarchal Basilica for the Patriarchate of Jerusalem in 451 AD with the Council of Chalcedon. [40] Santa Costanza is a church in Rome, built ca. 340-345 AD The building consists only of a rotunda. However, it is decisive that St. Michael's Church in Fulda (allegedly built from 820 to 822) is also a rotunda in the central structure. [41]

---

[39] Wikipedia (germ.) „Lateran – Gebäudekomplex in Rom" (called 26.6.2019)
[40] Wikipedia (germ.) „Sankt Laurentius vor den Mauern – Kirchengebäude in Rom" (called 26.6.2019)
[41] Wikipedia (germ.) „Santa Costanza – Kirchengebäude in Rom" (called 26.6.2019)

Trapezoid 2: Calculation of the parallelism (air lines 3 & 4)

How exactly is the air line Niederhadamar-Rom parallel to Fulda-Haddamar? One must probably go to Obervorschütz (instead of Haddamar). Furthermore, this line continues coming from Fulda on Niedenstein, Friedensstraße.

The coordinates of the places are:

P	X = East	Y = North	Village/Town
2	9.6727°	50.5538°	Fulda
4	9.2649°	51.1607°	Haddamar
4a	9.3138°	51.2300°	Niedenstein, Ziegenberg
4b	9.3530°	51.1622°	Obervorschütz
3	8.0346°	50.4355°	Niederhadamar
5	12.5059°	41.8866°	Rome Lateran
5a	12.5208°	41.9026°	Rome Laurentius
5b	12.5174°	41.9226°	Rome Constantia Grave

Here there are several places to choose from.

As the crow flies 3, coordinates of locations 2 and 4:

$$P_4 = \begin{pmatrix} x_4 \\ y_4 \end{pmatrix} \qquad P_2 = \begin{pmatrix} x_2 \\ y_2 \end{pmatrix}$$

As the crow flies 4, coordinates of locations 3 and 5:

$$P_3 = \begin{pmatrix} x_3 \\ y_3 \end{pmatrix} \qquad P_5 = \begin{pmatrix} x_5 \\ y_5 \end{pmatrix}$$

Ratios of coordinates are:

$$Ratio \ (air \ line \ 3) = \frac{\Delta \ Latitude}{\Delta \ Longitude} = \frac{(y_4 - y_2)}{(x_4 - x_2)}$$

$$Ratio\ (air\ line\ 4) = \frac{\Delta\ Latitude}{\Delta\ Longitude} = \frac{(y_3 - y_5)}{(x_3 - x_5)}$$

Then results (once written down in detail):

(Haddamar North – Fulda Dom North) / (Haddamar East – Fulda Dom East)
(51.1607° - 50.5538°) / (9.2649° - 9.6727°) = 0.6069° / - 0.4078° = *-1.4882*

Δ latitude/Δ longitude for this and other air lines (LL):

LL	Village/Town 1	Village/Town 2	Δ Lati /Δ Long
3	Haddamar	Fulda	1.4882 ≈ 1.49
3'	Niedenstein, Z.	Fulda	1.8841 ≈ 1.88
3''	Obervorschütz	Fulda	1.9030 ≈ 1.90
3'''	Forkenburg	Fulda	1.5619 ≈ 1.56
4	Niederhadamar	Rome, Lateran	1.9119 ≈ 1.91
4'	Niederhadamar	Rome, Laurentius	1.9020 ≈ 1.90
4''	Niederhadamar	Rome, Constantia	1.8990 ≈ 1.90

Conclusion:

- Christian buildings on the eastern edge of ancient Rome fit well

- Quotient becomes larger at point east of Haddamar (Obervorschütz)

- Parallelism is still good when using Haddamar

- Forkenburg (among others existing in the 10th century) slightly better than Haddamar

Other positions can be tried:

LL	Village/Town 1	Village/Town 2	Δ Lati /Δ Long
3'''	Metze	Fulda	1.9071 ≈ 1.91
	Wotanstein	Fulda	2.0182 ≈ 2.02
	Kassel, Fulda-Aue	Fulda	4.3126 ≈ 4.31
4'''	Niederhadamar	Rome, Pantheon	1.9217 ≈ 1.92
	Niederhadamar	Rome, Vatican Obelisk	1.9295 ≈ 1.93

- Conclusion:

- - Buildings in the west of Rome deviate too much

- - In Kassel you can see how quickly the quotient changes

=> Trapezoid 2 parallel Δ 8.4 km NNO Haddamar

Exact parallelism of the two air lines - in the west Niederhadamar-Rome and in the east Haddamar-Fulda - seems to result if one pushes the point from the village Haddamar near Fritzlar 8.4 kilometers away to the north-northeast. There lies the municipality of Niedenstein.

Note that the Rome-Hadamar route is more than twice as far as the Fulda-Langres route. Therefore, the deviation from the village of Haddamar near Fritzlar may be greater.
The creators of this construct of the two trapezoids (at the Altrhein they are even parallelograms) wanted to point in the first place to Langres in France, in the second place only to Rome. So my estimation. These trapezoids cannot be a coincidence. That was so wanted, I think.

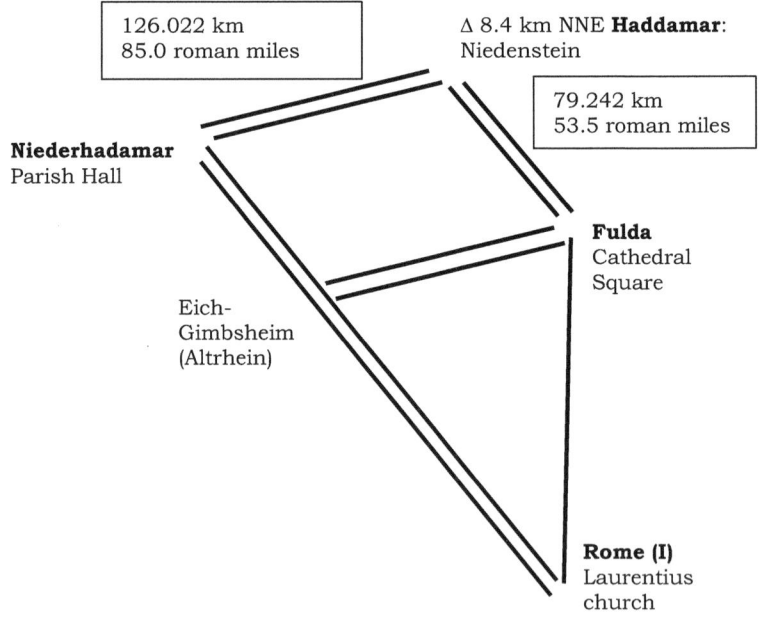

126.022 km
85.0 roman miles

Δ 8.4 km NNE **Haddamar:**
Niedenstein

79.242 km
53.5 roman miles

Niederhadamar
Parish Hall

Fulda
Cathedral
Square

Eich-
Gimbsheim
(Altrhein)

Rome (I)
Laurentius
church

168

Parallelogram 2: N'Hadamar (-Rom) to Eich-Gimbsheimer

Here we have two unknowns in the formula, because the north coordinate depends on the east coordinate and vice versa. We dissolve the formula after the north coordinate and set several east coordinates as a test. Then we look whether both coordinates are still in the area of the floodplain of the Kühkopf.

Kühkopf North = ((-1.9119 * (Kühkopf East – N'Hadamar East)) + N'Hadamar North
= (-1.9119 * (8.3720°- 8.0346°)) + 50.4355° = 49.79°

This position is located between Guntersblum and the current course of the Rhine, less than 2 km west of the Kühkopf floodplain.
With Fulda-Haddamar (Niedenstein), the Niederhadamar-Altrheinaue (Eich-Gimbsheim) line forms a parallelogram. There, on the Rheinaue, there is a point where the distances between the two overhead lines are the same. There the trapezoid becomes a parallelogram.

Altrhein: intersection N'Hadamar-Rome & Fulda-Langres

The intersection of the two airlines from Hesse to Rome and Langres can be calculated as follows.

The coordinates are:

P	X = East	Y = North	Village/Town
1	5.3348	47.8646	Langres
2	9.6727°	50.5538°	Fulda
3	8.0346°	50.4355°	Niederhadamar
5	12.5059°	41.8866°	Rome Lateran
5a	12.5208°	41.9026°	Rome Laurentius
5b	12.5174°	41.9226°	Rome Constantia Grave

As the crow flies 1, coordinates of locations 1 and 2:

$$P_1 = \begin{pmatrix} x_1 \\ y_1 \end{pmatrix} \qquad P_2 = \begin{pmatrix} x_2 \\ y_2 \end{pmatrix}$$

As the crow flies 3, coordinates of locations 3 and 5:

$$P_3 = \begin{pmatrix} x_3 \\ y_3 \end{pmatrix} \qquad P_5 = \begin{pmatrix} x_5 \\ y_5 \end{pmatrix}$$

Intersection with coordinates X(s) and Y(s):

$$S = \begin{pmatrix} x_s \\ y_s \end{pmatrix}$$

The appropriate formula to calculate the coordinates of the intersection point is:

$$x_s = \frac{(x_5 - x_3)(x_2 y_1 - x_1 y_2) - (x_2 - x_1)(x_5 y_3 - x_3 y_5)}{(y_5 - y_3)(x_2 - x_1) - (y_2 - y_1)(x_5 - x_3)}$$

$$y_s = \frac{(y_1 - y_2)(x_5 y_3 - x_3 y_5) - (y_3 - y_5)(x_2 y_1 - x_1 y_2)}{(y_5 - y_3)(x_2 - x_1) - (y_2 - y_1)(x_5 - x_3)}$$

$$x_s = 8.389$$

$$y_s = 49.758$$

This coordinate 49.758° North, 8.389° East is located at the Eich-Gimbsheimer Altrhein, more precisely at the northeast edge of the Elisabethensee. The lake lies between the Heinrichs-Talaue-See in the west and the Altrheinsee in the east. The lake is located about 2.7 km from the present straightened Rhine.
The calculation with the St. Laurentius Church in front of the wall in Rome and with the Constantia Mausoleum in

Rome should also give an intersection in these arms of the Old Rhine between Oppenheim and Worms. If the reader likes, he can calculate this.

Air lines N'Hadamar and Fulda intersect in Niedenstein

The intersection of the two air lines from a) Fulda and b) Niederhadamar, both of which could approximately meet in Niedenstein, can be calculated as follows.

The coordinates are:

P	X = East	Y = North	Village/Town
2	9.6727	50.5538	Fulda
4b	9.3530°	51.1622°	Obervorschütz
3	8.0346	50.4355	Niederhadamar
4a	9.3138°	51.2300°	Niedenstein

As the crow flies 3, coordinates of locations 2 and 4b:

$$P_2 = \begin{pmatrix} x_2 \\ y_2 \end{pmatrix} \qquad P_{4a} = \begin{pmatrix} x_{4b} \\ y_{4b} \end{pmatrix}$$

As the crow flies 2, coordinates of locations 3 and 4a:

$$P_3 = \begin{pmatrix} x_3 \\ y_3 \end{pmatrix} \qquad P_{4a} = \begin{pmatrix} x_{4a} \\ y_{4a} \end{pmatrix}$$

Intersection with coordinates X(s) and Y(s):

$$S = \begin{pmatrix} x_s \\ y_s \end{pmatrix}$$

The appropriate formula to calculate the coordinates of the intersection point is:

171

$$x_s = \frac{(x_{4a} - x_3)(x_{4b}y_2 - x_2y_{4b}) - (x_{4b} - x_2)(x_{4a}y_3 - x_3y_{4a})}{(y_{4a} - y_3)(x_{4b} - x_2) - (y_{4b} - y_2)(x_{4a} - x_3)}$$

$$y_s = \frac{(y_2 - y_{4b})(x_{4a}y_3 - x_3y_{4a}) - (y_3 - y_{4a})(x_{4b}y_2 - x_2y_{4b})}{(y_{4a} - y_3)(x_{4b} - x_2) - (y_{4b} - y_2)(x_{4a} - x_3)}$$

$x_s = 9.3162$

$y_s = 51.2301$

Thus, the intersection is almost near the previously assumed point in Niedenstein. Here we are east of the street "Am Ziegenberg", namely in the "Friedensstraße".

Fulda - Obervorschütz extends to Niedenstein

P	X = East	Y = North	Village/Town
2	9.6727°	50.5538°	Fulda
3	8.0346°	50.4355°	Niederhadamar
4a	9.3138°	51.2300°	Niedenstein
4b	9.3530°	51.1622°	Obervorschütz
4	9.2649°	51.1607°	Haddamar
4c	9.3347°	51.2056°	Metze
4d	9.6722°	50.5547°	Fulda, St. Michael

By how many degrees or kilometers does Niedenstein deviate from the axis Fulda - Obervorschütz?

For this we take the straight line equation in the plane and take the latitude of Niedenstein (Am Ziegenberg), which we have used before. Then we ask ourselves, which degree of longitude comes out and how large is the deviation to the degree of longitude used so far.

$$x = \frac{(x_2 - x_1)}{(y_2 - y_1)} * (y - y_1) + x_1$$

In the formula we put two points with known coordinates x_1,y_1 and x_2,y_2. Then we still know the latitude y of the third point. Then we calculate the nominal longitude x of the third point. Because only then the third point lies also on the straight line, thus same air line.

$$x = \frac{(9.3530 - 9.6727)}{(51.1622 - 50.5538)} * (51.2300 - 50.5538) + 9.6727$$

$$x = \frac{(-0.3195)}{(0.6084)} * (0.6762) + 9.6727$$

$$x = 0.3551 + 9.6727 = 9.3175$$

The difference between actual (x) and target (x) is then:
9.3138 - 9.3175 = -0.0037°

One degree of longitude has about 70 kilometers at 50° northern latitude.
So in kilometers it would be:
0.0037° * 70 = 259 meters deviation, which is still within the locality of Niedenstein.

Haddamar - Deviations from air lines

The deviation from Niederhadamar-Niedenstein is 4.4 km.
The deviation from Fulda-Obervorschütz (and Niedenstein)
is 6.1 km.

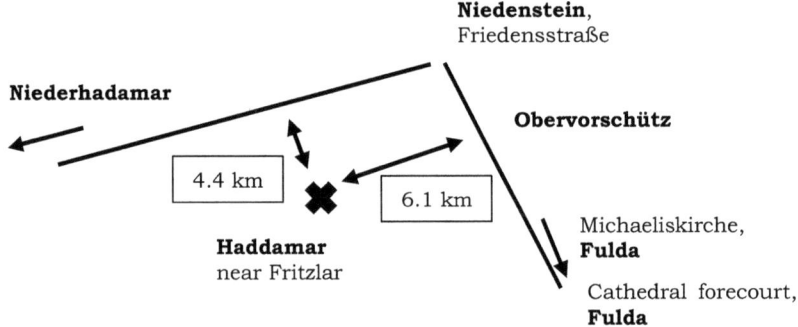

The axis from the southwestern cathedral forecourt in Fulda
to Haddamar also runs through the Michaeliskirche in
Fulda. This can probably also not be a coincidence.

Ancient cities on a line

If you draw lines with a pencil on the map of Europe I use,
the following cities, for example, seem to lie (roughly) on a
line:

a) Tours – Nîmes – Arles – Karthago (Tunis)
b) Tours – Langres – Vienna
c) Hadamar (near Limburg a.d. Lahn) – Bologna – Rome
d) Haddamar (near Fritzlar) – Fulda – Augsburg – Venice
    – Naples
e) Rome – Pergamon – Antiochia

Earth not a perfect sphere: Berlin-Lisbon and Berlin-Tokyo

In the previous subchapters we had calculated with coordinates. They should be unique for a point on the earth. Even if the earth is not a perfect sphere, every coordinate can - I think - be projected onto a sphere. Different heights above or below sea level can be "extrapolated" to any sphere. It looks a little bit different, if one wants to calculate the distances between two points on the earth as in the following subchapters. The earth is not a perfect sphere.

A perfect sphere would result in the following distances, for example:
Berlin Brandenburg Gate - Lisbon Tejo Bridge = 2318 km [42]
Berlin (52.517° N, 13.40° O) – Tokio (35.70° N, 139.767° O) = 8918 km [43]
(Berlin Castle) - (Post Office north of Gundam Cafe)

If one uses the reference ellipsoid, then result in distances:
Berlin Brandenburg Gate - Lisbon Tejo Bridge = 2335 km [44]

Berlin (52.517° N, 13.40° O) – Tokio (35.70° N, 139.767° O) = 8941 km [45]
This results in a difference of: Δ 17 km and Δ 23 km.

Google Maps states:
Berlin Brandenburg Gate - Lisbon Tejo Bridge = 2315 km
Berlin (52.517° N, 13.40° O) – Tokio (35.70° N, 139.767° O) = 8919 km
If the coordinates are correct, then Google Maps uses a sphere.

---

[42] www.kompf.de/gps/distcalc.html (called 8.5.2019)
[43] Wikipedia (germ.) „Orthodrome" (called 8.5.2019)
[44] www.kompf.de/gps/distcalc.html (called 8.5.2019)
[45] Wikipedia (germ.) „Orthodrome" (called 8.5.2019)

The orthodrome (Greek orthos for "straight", dromos for "run") is the shortest connection between two points on a spherical surface. It is usually referred to as a straight line. Aircraft fly on an orthodrome only at the equator. At the north and south poles it is tilted 90 degrees against the equatorial ring.

The air line from Fulda to Haddamar (Fritzlar) has about 73 km on a sphere. According to the rule of three x = 17 * 73 / 2318 the distance on an ellipsoid "Lisbon" could be extended by good 500 meters. "Tokyo" would be just under 200 meters with x = 23 * 73 / 8918.
The distance Göttingen-Mannheim, which was calculated at the beginning of the 19th century, is a few 100 meters longer compared to the sphere. [46]

1.5 Roman Miles = 1 Roman League

Roman Miles: 1.48176 km

Five foot lengths are a double step, that is, a "passus".
A thousand "passi" are one Roman mile.
According to a Wikipedia page, the Roman mile is 1480 meters. The mile is calculated from the foot length of 296 millimeters. [47]
Another source takes the foot length more exactly with 296.352 millimeters. This results in 1482 meters for the Roman mile. Strictly speaking, 296.352 times 5 equals 1481.76 meters or 1.48176 kilometers. [48]

---

[46] Different books on https://books.google.de (called 8.5.2019)
[47] Wikipedia (germ.) „Alte Maße und Gewichte (Römische Antike)" (called 23.5.2019)
[48] www.hellenicaworld.com/Italy/RomanEmpire/LX/de/RoemischeMasseGewichte.html (called 23.5.2019)

Miles of air lines from Fulda - "Measure distance"

From the Fulda cathedral place (northern end of the way "Domplatz" in Google Maps) to the thoroughfare "Züschener Straße" in Haddamar near Fritzlar is 73.33 km. That is 73.33 / 1.48176 = 49.49 Roman miles, or about 49.5 Roman miles.

From the cathedral square in Fulda to the street "Am Ziegenberg" in Niedenstein (eastern side), the distance according to Google Maps is 79.24 km. That makes about 53.5 roman miles. In contrast to the distance to Haddamar, this is not too striking a number. However, the parallelism of the routes seems to be better.

From the northern end of Domplatzstrasse in Fulda to the center of the cathedral in Langres is 434.29 km, according to Google Maps. This corresponds to 293.1 rom. miles.

Miles of air lines from Niederhadamar - "Measure distance"

The distance from Haddamar near Fritzlar to Niederhadamar is given by Google Maps as 118.22 km. That is 79.78 Roman miles.

The distance from the community center in Niederhadamar to the street "Am Ziegenberg" (eastern side) in Niedenstein is 126.022 km according to Google Maps.

That makes in Roman miles with the factor 1.48176 approx. 85 Roman miles.

To Langres it makes a distance according to Google Maps of 346.78 km. That makes in Roman miles with the factor 1.48176 then 234.03 Roman miles.

This is an interesting distance because the digits run up from 2 to 4.

From the center in Niederhadamar (parish hall) to the Lateran Palace in Rome is about 1010 km. That is about 682 Roman miles.

Fulda-Haddamar: exactly 33 Roman Leagues

While the Roman mile consists of 5000 feet (pedes), the Roman leuge (Latin: Leuga, Leuca) has 7500 feet. The measure of length "leuge" was used only in the Roman northwestern provinces. Preserved are for example the leuge stones from Mainz-Kastel to Wiesbaden and from Bingen to Trier. [49]
Conversion: 1 leuca = 1.5 Roman miles = 1.5 x 1.48176 km = 2.22264 km.

Surprisingly, 49.50 Roman miles, i.e. as the crow flies between Fulda Domplatz (northern end of the path "Domplatz" according to Google Maps) and the village of Haddamar (through road to Züschen in the west and Werkel in the east), result in exactly 33.00 Roman leugen.
It is 49.50 Roman miles / 1.5 = 33.00 Roman leugen.
In kilometers, this is exactly: 73.34712 km (49.50 x 1.48176).

Under a) the idealized condition that the earth is a perfect sphere (because Google Maps seems to reckon with that), and with b) the starting point Villa Rustica in Fulda (at the northern end path "Domplatz" at 50.5538° North, 9.6727° East) one comes c) in the village Haddamar to within 10 meters exactly on the through road "Züschener Straße", which runs in east-west direction (north of the old village) from Werkel to Züschen. That is exactly 33.00 Roman leugen. At this place in Haddamar the coordinates are at 51.1610° North and 9.2646° East.

---

[49] Wikipedia (en) League, ancient distance (called 30.8.2019)

Age of Jesus at 33 years

Jesus of Nazareth is said to have been born in 4 BC and died in 30 or 31 AD. Often in the early church an age of 33 years is given. [50] A clue for his year of death is possibly the 3-hour lunar eclipse at the crucifixion of Jesus. [51] There are lunar eclipses in the years around 30 AD which fit locally only approximately. (Approx.) 297 years later, on 29.4.329, there was a total lunar eclipse which fits better. [52] Is it possible to utilize this somehow?

Adalbert Feltz wrote: According to this, the birth of Jesus Christ would have to be assigned to the year 292/93 AD in the calendar valid for us today, by the way in brilliant agreement with the Great Conjunction of Jupiter and Saturn as the Star of Bethlehem, which turned out to be much more impressive at that time than 7 BC The connection of the conjunction of 7 BC with the star of Bethlehem and the birth of Christ was brought into discussion and spread by J. Kepler as is known. [53]

Dr. Heribert Illig points in connection with the presumed phantom time of 297 years = 11 x 3 x 3 between 614 and 911 AD to the age of Jesus Christ of 33 years at his crucifixion favored in the early Christian church. [54]

Also traded with the number "33" is the year in which the man converted from Saul to Paul is said to have started his missionary activity. [55]

---

[50] Wikipedia (germ.) „Jesus von Nazaret – jüdischer Wanderprediger (called 10.9.2019)

[51] Wikipedia (germ.) „Finsternis bei der Kreuzigung Jesu"

[52] https://www.der-mond.org/mondfinsternis/...

[53] http://www.adalbert-feltz.at/2017/03/23/die-realitaet-der-mittelalterlichen-phantomzeit-und-ihre-konsequenzen/

[54] Illig: Wer hat an der Uhr gedreht, S.19 und S.176

[55] Wikipedia (germ.) „Paulus von Tarsus – Apostel und Missionar des Urchristentums" (called 11.9.2019)

Calculation distance Fulda to Haddamar

On the plain: 33.02 Roman Leagues

We can roughly calculate the distance between Fulda and Haddamar if we assume a plane (and not a globe) for such a short distance (relative to the entire earth). We use it to calculate Euclidean.

The coordinates - mentioned above - are:

Villa Rustica, Fulda: 50.5538° North, 9.6727° East
Haddamar, Züschener Straße: 51.1610° N, 9.2646° E

The difference in latitude is then:

$$\Delta \text{Latitude} = (51.1610° - 50.5538°) = 0.6072°$$

The distance of 1 ° latitude on the globe corresponds to 111.3 km.

$$\Delta \text{Latitude} = 0.6072° * 111.3 \frac{km}{°} = 67.58 \, km$$

The difference in longitude is then:

$$\Delta \, Longitude = (9.6727° - 9.2646°) = 0.4081°$$

The distance A between two degrees of longitude depends on the degree of latitude. The formula is:

$$A = cos \, \varphi * 2 * \frac{R}{360}$$

R is the radius of the earth (depending on the latitude) and φ the latitude.

The mean latitude of the two places Fulda and Haddamar is:

$$(50.5538° + 51.1610°) / 2 = 50.8574°$$

This results in an earth radius of: 6365.3 km

Formula and input options with automatic calculation are offered, for example, on the website "rechneronline.de". At the equator it is 6,378.1 km and at the poles it is 6,356.8 km. The earth is not a perfect sphere.

This results in the distance of 1 ° longitude at 50.86 ° latitude as:

$$A = cos\ 50.8574° * 2 * \frac{6365.3}{360}$$

$$A = 70.128\ km$$

Because of the difference of 0.4081 °, which was calculated above, these are then:

$$\Delta\,Longitude = 0.4081° * 70.128\,\frac{km}{°} = 28.62\,km$$

According to the Pythagorean theorem in the right-angled triangle, the distance between Fulda and Haddamar then results:

$$\Delta\,(FH) = \sqrt[2]{(\Delta\,\text{Latitude})^2 + (\Delta\,Longitude)^2} =$$

$$\sqrt[2]{(67.58\,km)^2 + (28.62\,km)^2} = 73.39\,km$$

That is 73.39 / 1.48176 = 49.53 Roman miles and 33.02 Roman leagues.

On the globe: 32.97 Roman Leagues

The formula for calculating the beeline is:
$$cos(G) =$$

$$sin(lat1) * sin(lat2) + cos(lat1) * cos(lat2) * cos(lon2 - log1)$$

in which
G = great arc
Latitude = latitude = lat
Longitude = longitude = lon

The coordinates - mentioned above - are again:

Villa Rustica, Fulda: 50.5538° North, 9.6727° East
Haddamar, Züschener Straße: 51.1610° N, 9.2646° E

A pocket calculator calculates here with the coordinates in degrees.
However, Excel calculates with the radians, i.e. with the factor

$$Coordinate\ in\ radians = coordinate\ in\ degrees * \frac{\pi}{180°}$$

This results in radians:

Villa Rustica, Fulda: 0.88233 rad N, 0.16882 rad E
Haddamar, Züschener Str.:0.89293 rad N, 0.16170 rad E

This results in $cos(G) = 0.999933738$

Now you have to take the arccos from it and multiply it by the radius of the earth.
The mean radius of the earth was calculated as: 6365.3 km

$$\Delta\,(FH) = 6365.3 * arccos(G) = 73.277\ km$$

That is 73.28 / 1.48176 = 49.45 Roman miles and 32.97 Roman leagues.

When calculating a) in the plane or b) on the sphere, the distance is very close to 33 Roman leagues.

Both calculations are made at sea level. The places are on average at approx. 240 meters. The radius of the earth should actually be increased by this amount.

Parallelism Rome, Langres, Fulda, Had(d)amar

Distance Fulda - Haddamar: 33 Leagues: own calculations

The distance between the positions Fulda (Domplatz or Villa Rustica) and Haddamar (thoroughfare) is almost exactly 33 Roman Leugen. 1 Leuga (Leuca) = 1.5 Roman miles = 2.22264 kilometers. However, the earth is not a perfect sphere. But at a distance of "only" around 70 kilometers, the deviations are in a range of a few 100 meters. The question is what the designer of this distance relied on. Perhaps he, too, had expected the perfect ball.

Comment on parallelism

In the approach I put the coordinates (length, width) in relation to get a measure of the parallelism. It is clear, however, that the longitudes are spaced ever smaller towards the pole. The latitudes have constant distances. Of the great circle that forms the equator, only small circles on the globe are used to the north and south. The calculations above would look a little different if one also had the longitudes not only on great circles, but also used small circles. The longitudes are not parallel. Nevertheless, I spoke of parallelism above. The line from Fulda towards Haddamar near Fritzlar would run even further to the east (east of Niedenstein) with parallel longitudes. The question is what the designer was working with in the early Middle Ages.

Height differences between Langres and Haddamar

Another point would be the differences in altitude between Langres, Fulda, Haddamar and Niederhadamar. Langres is the highest, Niederhadamar the lowest.
If one imagines a table top that has to be tilted (and thus "pulls" closer to Haddamar), then the effect is in the 100 meter range, certainly not more than 8 km between Niedenstein and Haddamar. In addition, Haddamar would have to be the lowest point at Fritzlar, which is not the case.
The city of Langres is located on a mountain and on average 468 meters above sea level. [56] The district is between 327 and 475 meters above sea level. [57]
(NN. (In 1993, NN or N.N. was replaced by NHN "normal height zero") Haddamar near Fritzlar is 215 meters above sea level. [58]
Niederhadamar near Limburg a.d. Lahn is 134 meters above sea level in the center of the village. NN. The district varies between 120 and 235 meters. [59]
Fulda is located at 261 meters above sea level. [60]

---

[56] Wikipedia (fr.) „Langres – commune française du département de la Haute-Marne" (called 31.8.2019)
[57] Wikipedia (germ.) „Langres – französische Gemeinde" (called 31.8.2019)
[58] Wikipedia (germ.) „Haddamar – Stadtteil von Fritzlar" (called 31.8.2019)
[59] Wikipedia (germ.) „Niederhadamar – Stadtteil von Hadamar" (called 31.8.2019)
[60] Wikipedia (germ.) „Fulda – Kreisstadt im Landkreis Fulda in Hessen mit Sonderstatus" (called 31.8.2019)

Germanicus near Niedenstein (+ with 33 years)

Germanicus (* May 24th, 2015 BC, + October 10th, 19 AD in Antioch) was the nephew of Tiberius and the father of Caligula. He destroyed in 15 AD the Chattic place Mattium, which is supposed to be in this area. The town of Metze between Niedenstein and Gudensberg and the town of Maden near Gudensberg, where the Wotansstein stands, sound similar in this area. The Matzoff stream flows through Metze. [61]

The question is whether I started wrong with the parallelism of the air lines and whether the parallelism goes through Haddamar at Fritzlar. If not, did the designer of these distances and parallels want to refer to Germanicus?

He died at the age of 15 + 19 - 1 = 33 years.
(-1 because the year zero does not exist). [62]

---

[61] Wikipedia (germ.) „Mattium" (called 9.8.2019)
[62] Wikipedia (germ.) „Germanicus – römischer Feldherr, Adoptivsohn des Kaisers Tiberius" (called 13.9.2019)

This is roughly what the Hatto window looks like.
Original window in the Cathedral Museum in Mainz.
Previously installed in a house in Weintorstrasse 11.
(LVX ET S)AL before HATTHO can be detected weakly. There
is a slight "S", "FT" etc. The copy is not quite correct.

Points of contact with Langres and Rome

Andematunnum (Langres) and Hademar

In my german written book "Die verfälschte Antike" from 2013 I had already pointed out that because of the diplomacy of Abbot Hadamar (+956) between the Germanic Ottonians and the Pope in Rome, the Hadamar family could come from a Gallo-Roman family.
Langres (between Dijon and Toul) was called Andematunnum in the old Roman Empire. Can Hademar be deduced from this?
The personal name Hademar or Hadamar could be a play on words with the ancient Roman name of the French city of Langres.

Hatto, Hadamar: Diplomats for German kings and popes

Abbot Hadamar was in Rome four times on behalf of the Ottonians. But his nephew Hatto II also had contacts there. Perhaps related to both of them, Hatto III, Abbot of Fulda (+997) was also used to mediate the coronation of Otto III. Sent by Adelheid of Burgundy, the third wife of Otto I, to the Pope in Rome. Here I suspect a very good relationship with the powerful in Rome, which perhaps had existed generations before.

Vocal and consonant play Attalos to (H-) Attamar?

When changing from the Greek name Attalos to the Roman name Attalus, there was only the vowel change from "o" to "u".
If you want to camouflage the name because Roman family names from the 6th or 10th century AD are frowned upon, then it would make sense to let the last vowel in the name wander one more vowel in the alphabet. "U" then becomes "a". In addition, you change two consonants around this

vowel. The consonant BEFORE the last vowel is set one position further back in the alphabet and the consonant AFTER the last vowel is set one position further forward in the alphabet, ie "L" to "M" and "S" to "R", then one would have made an "Attamar" out of "Attalus". Is that a coincidence or an intention?

Attalus – Attalus – Attamar

O –U – A Vowel: +1, +1 "from the front" with A
L – M consonant 1: +1 in the alphabet high
S – R Consonant 2: -1 lower in the alphabet

Abbot Hadamar's references to Hattons

Hatto II (+970), Abbot Hadamar's nephew, and Otto I.

• Abbot of Fulda 956 to 968
• Archbishop of Mainz 968 to 970

According to the chronicler Marianus Scotus (* 1028 in Ireland, +1082/83 in Mainz), Hatto II was the son of the sister of Abbot Hadamar von Fulda.
First Hatto II was a monk in Fulda, then a priest. He was a participant in Hadamar's first trip to Rome in 936. He became abbot on 7/28/956. Stays at the royal court are recorded for 961 with Otto I (the elder) and 967 with Otto II (* 955, +983 in Rome).
In 961 he traveled to Rome on behalf of Otto I to prepare for the imperial coronation, at which he was present in 962. 961 the privileges of the monastery by Pope John XII. approved. After March 2, 968, Hatto II. raised as the successor of Wilhelm to Archbishop of Mainz. Hatto very much accommodated the wishes of Emperor Otto I when the Archdiocese of Magdeburg was founded.
He died on January 18, 970. [63]

Hatto III. (+997) and Otto's wife Adelheid and Otto III.

• Abbot of Fulda 991 to 997

Hatto III. was a monk since 987 and abbot in Fulda since 991. 994 was Hatto by Pope John XV. (985-996) ordained abbot. Stays at the royal court with Otto III. (* 980 for Kleve, +1002 for Faleria) are occupied for 994 and 995. The abbot led embassies on behalf of Otto III. to Rome, in 994 to Pope

---

[63] Schmid: Die Klostergemeinschaft von Fulda im frühen Mittelalter, Band 1, S.191

John XV. and 997 to Pope Gregory V. He died on April 25, 997. [64]

Hatto III. had only been a monk in the Fulda monastery for four years when he was elected abbot of the monastery in 991 and was given by King Otto III. was used. In September 994 he took part in the Reichstag in Sohlingen (part of the city of Uslar, district of Northeim, Lower Saxony; not Solingen in North Rhine-Westphalia), at which the 14-year-old king was declared of legal age. Hatto received the order, Pope John XV. to inform about the resolutions of the Reichstag. [...] He seems to have been the first abbot to be ordained by the Pope. On October 31, 994, John XV confirmed him. the privileges of his predecessors and allowed him to wear the dalmatic and sandals at mass.

On March 31, 1995, Hatto III, who probably negotiated with the Pope on behalf of the king, also about his imperial coronation, stayed again with Otto in Nijmegen.

In February 997 Hatto took part in a synod in Pavia. There, Pope Gregory V confirmed him the privilege of wearing cardinal robes, i.e. dalmatic and sandals, at mass. [65]

A relationship with Hatto II is not known. It can only be assumed because of a) a similarly important task, which consisted of negotiating the imperial coronation between the German king and the Pope in Rome, b) the same office as abbot in Fulda and c) the name "Hatto".

The rise and fall of the Hattons in the 10th century AD

After the Ottonians from Lower Saxony had obviously become aware of the Hattons through the rebellion of Konrad from the Lahngau, they had not only sent this family to Rome as negotiating partner for the incumbent popes. The kings Heinrich I and Otto I had used the services of Abbots

---

[64] Schmid: Die Klostergemeinschaft von Fulda im frühen Mittelalter, Band 1, S.193

[65] Leinweber: Die Fuldaer Äbte und Bischöfe, S.36

Hadamar (927-956) and Hatto II (956-968) of Fulda. After that, it became quiet around the family for the time being.

Otto II, who married the Byzantine princess Theophanu, could (and this is only an assumption) have disapproved of the extraordinary position of the Hattons and preferred to have recourse to the support of the then Archbishop of Cologne.

When Otto II died prematurely, and his son Otto III. was still a minor, remembered Adelheid, the third and last wife of Otto I and his widow probably of the Hattons and demanded Hatto III. (+997), Abbot of Fulda, to organize an imperial coronation for her grandson in Rome.

Hatto III. As an abbot, he had received very special rights from the Pope, which was also reflected in his clothing. He was the leading abbot in Germany.

Adelheid also descended from the Burgundian rulers, which is certainly not entirely insignificant for their relationship with the Hattons, if one could assume that the Hattons come from Burgundy.

However, Hatto III died. on his return trip to Fulda.

The importance of the Hattons died out with the death of Hatto III. in 997 AD (also) suddenly in Germany.

The question with the Hattons is why they were used to negotiate the imperial title for the German royal house from Lower Saxony twice (Otto I and Otto III) with the Pope in Rome. Did the family perhaps once hold an imperial title and was therefore predestined to do so?

If the Hattons were Gallo-Romans, then for this reason they would have had a suitable reference to Italy. Few Gallo-Roman families, as church dignitaries, have great influence among the Merovingians. A Sidonius from Auvergne is bishop of Mainz in the 6th century and is perhaps related to Sidonius Apollinaris from Clermont (-Ferrand).

Pallium 896 (Mainz) & 599 (Autun) - "297"

In 599 the Bishop of Autun received the right to wear the pallium from Pope Gregory the Elder. Major (tenure 590-604). [66] The bishop's name was Syagrius and his tenure was from around 560 to 600. [67]

Bishop Hatto I of Mainz receives the pallium from Pope Formosus on his second trip to Rome (from autumn 895 to spring 896). [68]

599 and 896 are the same year if the time between 614 and 911 did not exist, i.e. 297 = 11 x 3 x 3 x 3 years difference. That would be - taking into account the "phantom time" (Dr. H. Illig) - perhaps a further indication that the Hattons come from Burgundy. Both bishops had received from Pope Gregory the Great. got the pallium in the same year.

---

[66] http://www.newadvent.org/cathen/02144.htm (called 20.7.2002); in this: Georges Goyau, Thomas J. Shahan: „Autun" in Catholic Encyclopedia (1999) including use of the source: DIOCESE: Gallia Christiana ed nova (1728), IV, 314-437 und Dokumente, 39-126

[67] Wikipedia (germ.) „Liste der Bischöfe von Autun" (called 14.7.2019)

[68] https://www.cathlinks.com/hatto/ (called 13.7.2019); in this: Michael Ott including use of the sources: Dammert, Hatto I. Erzbischof von Mainz in Freiburger Programm (1864, 1865) and others
http://www.newadvent.org/cathen/07149c.htm (called 4.12.2001); in this: Michael Ott (same information as under „cathlinks")

Archaeological finds in Fulda 6.-10. Century

Do the Hattons match the findings or not? The following subsections could be seen under this point. They are almost exclusively quoted verbatim.

Grave of Otto, Islamic faience, sandstone head

The Fulda of the 10th century has

a) in a grave a lead plate with the text "OTTO XPI AN DE PAGANO O NO OCT", [69]

b) Islamic luster faience [70] (from diplomats?) and

c) to present an artfully made head made of sandstone (approx. 8 cm high, approx. 4 cm wide). [71]

To a) The lead plaque is in a showcase in the Fulda Cathedral Museum. It is very green, the lead is flaking off. Translated, the inscription means: "Otto, became a Christian from a pagan, died of the nuns of October." The lead tablet was found in a sarcophagus with a lid (early Romanesque, sandstone). The coffin was found next to the royal chapel of the collegiate church in Fulda. It is said to be a relative of the Ottonian royal family. About the coffin of approx. 8 coffins on the east side of today's predecessor building of the Fulda Cathedral it says elsewhere: "A stone coffin stood 2.5 m east of the chapel [.]" And further: "The undisturbed burial is a male skeleton 1.75 m in length and moderately strong bone structure; the skull is already badly

---

[69] Nicht: Das Dommuseum Fulda, S.31
[70] Ludowici: Frühmittelalterliche islamische Fayence aus Fulda, in: Germania 72, S. 612
[71] Nicht: Das Dommuseum Fulda, S.23 (Comment: a different perspective of the head in: Dommuseum, short guide through the exhibition)

deformed; the rows of teeth are closed, the wisdom teeth well developed. [...] Under the cervical vertebrae there was a 24 x 26.5 cm sheet of lead, heavily oxidized, with the following inscription: [...] "(see above)" A woolen ring band lies around the thigh above the right knee of the buried person. Any clues about the personality have not been gained to this day. " 72

Ancient Roman construction in Fulda 1: The three rooms

<u>1a) Prof. Dr. Joseph Vonderau writes:</u>
"However, the experimental trenches set radially from the exposed east apse in pursuit of this presumed older upper cloister led to another interesting building complex. To the southeast of the old church buildings, the areas of two rooms were completely exposed and a third room in its eastern part was still reached. Since the north-western foundation walls of these rooms run under the building from 791, they must have been built before 791. In view of the great age of these systems, particular care was taken to uncover them. The three rooms do not lie at the same time as all of the old baselines that have been determined up to now, but rather intersect the axis of the church with their longitudinal direction at an oblique angle. [] "
In the chapter it is further reported what kind of materials were used, that because of the dampness one did without a basement and put in a drainage. After all, it says: "The whole technique of this "brick terrazzo" is Roman. This finding cannot come as a surprise and it must not lead to false conclusions regarding the builder of these "cells"; because the Fulda monastery is also reported to have built more romano there and eagerly studied the writings of the Roman architect Vitruvius." 73

---

72 Vonderau: Die Ausgrabungen am Dome zu Fulda usw. 1908-1913, S.28f.
73 Vonderau: Die Ausgrabungen am Dome zu Fulda usw. 1908-1913, S.5ff.

1b) In the book "Hessen in the Early Middle Ages Archeology and Art" is written:
"The three cells lie diagonally in front of the south tower of the cathedral as the remainder of a larger building, the western outline of which cannot be grasped because it is now overbuilt by the cathedral. It was a stone building with 0.70 to 0.75 m thick, 0.20 m recessed walls. Three rooms are connected one behind the other: Room I measured inside 6 m long and 4.40 m wide, room II just as wide and 8 m long, room III also 4.40 m wide, the length is no longer tangible. The brick terrazzo floor was striking. Experts referred to him as "Roman". But in 1919 it was thought to be an early monastery. The walls were covered with smooth plaster. The remains of a heating system were found in cell II, but the construction method could not be determined in detail. There were cracked and sooty bricks as the remains of a heating duct.
Unfortunately, the excavation here hardly revealed any finds. The wall plaster had remains of painting and writing, but this was probably a testimony to its use in monastic times. So also the gold strip, the edge of a glass beaker like a piece of ivory, probably coming from a stick (Vonderau 1924). " [74]

Antique-Roman construction in Fulda 2: The angular construction

2) In the book "Hessen im Frühmittelalter Archäologie und Kunst" is written:
"Since the excavations at Domplatz were cut into walls that did not harmonize with those of the monastery in the same direction as the three cells and walls that came out in 1928, it was decided in 1941 that an excavation should be carried out in view of the 1200th anniversary in 1944. With a different direction than the three cells, a building with five

---

[74] Roth, Wamers (Editor): Hessen im Frühmittelalter Archäologie und Kunst, S.301

rooms was seized on the south side of the Domplatz, which was obviously laid out at an angle, with the courtyard part facing the Waidesbach.

Room 1: Enclosed on the outside by 70 cm thick walls, it was 6 m long and 6.50 m wide. On the eastern gable wall there were two rows of post holes from a previous period with Chattic shards of the Roman Empire.
The south wall towards the brook was subsequently supported by three buttresses.
On the floor there was painted wall plaster in the colors orange, wine-red, beige and gray-blue.

Room 2: [...] 6.50 m long and 7 m long. Secondary fireplaces in three corners with coal, ash and slag from the monastery era. In contrast, a fragment of a Hallstatt bronze bracelet and a narrow strip of gold were found here.
A piece of wall was traced on the south-west corner, which points to an intangible, adjoining room to the south. On this wall there was a denarius of Louis the Pious [...], a further indication of a secondary use of this building in the monastery period.

Room 3: It continues at room 2 to the west with a width of 6.50 m. Length not determined, probably 9.50 m
Corner room: not excavated. The internal dimensions can be determined by the alignment of the wall at 6.50 m by 6.70 m. The corner of the Sturmius monastery is to be found here.
In a second excavation area, the course of the walls encountered in 1928 was followed and led to the partial investigation of rooms 4 and 5.

Room 4: Here, too, the width of the walls is 70 cm. Partition wall 60 cm. The excellent floor screed was found at a depth of 4.35 m under the Domplatz. The interior dimensions of the room are to be reconstructed: 6.70 m wide and 8 m long.

On the floor lay sigillata shards and pieces of vessels from the Merovingian era, over which stone slabs were laid on which the cultural layer of the monastery period lay. An oak stake from the pre-Merovingian era was found under the screed.

Room 5: The length of this room is not recorded, the width is 6.70 m. The equally excellent screed floor was here at a depth of 4.19 m. There was a heating device in this room. It was a slab layer characterized by the effects of fire. The screed above also showed the effects of heat below. The remaining heating system was connected to room 4 by a canal. It is considered to be the oldest heating system from the Merovingian era found in Germany on the right bank of the Rhine.

Walls: The construction of the walls sunk into the ground was uniform, as the two lowest layers were often columnar basalts without mortar bedding, on which the mortar wall sat. This method turned out to be beneficial drainage.

Covering: For the wrapped building, ledge bricks like hollow bricks were used, they were introduced [from somewhere else] as a material investigation showed.

Floor: The floor height is given for rooms 4 and 5. 4.19 and 4.35 m depth below the Domplatz level. No information is available for rooms 1 to 3.

Profile: Of decisive importance for this excavation was the profile that was found in room 4, reaching down to a depth of 5 m. A Chattic period with wooden buildings was followed without interruption by the Merovingian with stone buildings. It was destroyed by fire. The layer of fire is covered with stone slabs as a base for the cultural layers of the monastery period. It was thus proven that there was previously a settlement on the monastery area that had stone buildings. Research results that have often been overlooked, although there have been no Merovingian stone buildings and heating systems east of the Rhine so far.

The find material comes from three periods, such as the Roman Empire with indigenous Chatti ceramics. There are also imported Roman goods (Terra Sigillata and Terra Nigra). Franconian-Merovingian vessel fragments come from the second epoch, from the third Carolingian ware from the monastery period.
In addition to several metal objects, the fragment of a sandstone capital with an Ionic volute and a stylized piece of palmette [...] and a bronze pen from the monastic period [...] and a denarius of Louis the Pious deserve special mention. [...]
The main excavation result compared to the earlier idea is: In the monastic area there is a pre-monastery, Merovingian period, the stone buildings of which were destroyed by fire. The monastery used the old buildings by restoring the parts, at least until the completion of the monastery founded in 744. The settlement gap, vastitudo, is likely to have been around 30 years (Vonderau 1946). " [75]

Antique Roman construction in Fulda 3: The palace building

3a) In the "Handbuch der Deutschen Kunstdenkmäler, Hessen" it says:
"Fulda: Old prehistoric settlement, finds from the Stone, Bronze and Iron Ages. In Franconian times (6th century) a fortified, shield-shaped Curtis was built, probably as the administrative center of Buchonia (Buchenland, western part of the Grabfeldgau).
A palace-like, perhaps two-storey building with six rooms (17.65 m x 32.75 m) in the style of the Roman villa rustica,

---

[75] Roth, Wamers (Editor): Hessen im Frühmittelalter Archäologie und Kunst, S.301f.

an angular house with underfloor heating and another rectangular building excavated under the cathedral square. The complex was destroyed in the Saxon Wars at the end of the 7th century and not rebuilt.

744 Foundation of a Benedictine monastery by St. Sturmius (from Bavaria, +779) on behalf of his teacher, St. Boniface, who made the richly endowed monastery the main base for the Christianization of Central Germany [...]." [76]

3b) In the book "Hessen im Frühmittelalter Archäologie und Kunst" is written:

"In preparation for the 1200th anniversary of Boniface in 1954, the Domplatz was to be redesigned. So in 1953 the opportunity arose to examine this area with the aim of clarifying the question of the palace structure and to follow the sloping wall on which Otto's sarcophagus had stood.

It was possible to grasp the lines of the walls of the younger paradise as well as those of the older paradise. The inclined wall belonged to a pre-monastery period and was a large building oriented towards the Waides, which was designed as a stone building according to the type of villa rustica of the Romans.

There was no cultural layer, as the more recent periods each laid the floors lower than their predecessors, as was shown by leveling the floor heights - the break point from the foundation to the rising masonry. That is why this excavation brought hardly any dating finds.

The large rectangular stone building had six rooms. A pergola of two square rooms was set in front, behind which a large hall was flanked by two rectangular rooms. An upper floor is conceivable. Unfortunately, no underfloor heating could be detected here because the floors were no longer there. The building is to be oriented towards the Waides flowing past. The foundation of the walls was usually 1.10

---

[76] Dehio, Gall: Handbuch der Deutschen Kunstdenkmäler, Hessen, S. 293

m wide, the walls on top were 60 to 70 cm thick. The front southern wall showed the lower stone layers of the foundation unmorted, as was already observed in the other Merovingian buildings. The upper foundation layers like the walls are mortar walls.

The dimensions of the large building, known as the "palace": length 32.75 m, width 17.65 m.

Front: Pergola, flush with the line, length 17.30 m, depth 5.95 m. West corner room almost square, width 5.85 m, depth 5.60 m. East corner room almost square, width 5.50 m, depth 5.75 m. Main part of the building, the hall immediately behind the pergola: Hall length 18 m, depth 8.35 m. Western flanking area: width 5.75 m, depth 8.45 m. Eastern flanking area: width 4.90 m , Depth 8.30 m. The U-shaped wall found in the main room as in the pergola indicates a secondary use of this building after restoration in the early monastic period.

This palace building bears witness to the survival of Roman building forms in the Merovingian period up to the Carolingian era, probably carried by builders on the left bank of the Rhine. In the Merovingian core area, such buildings were continued, especially in the Palatinate. That is why one can see a Merovingian Palatinate in Eihloha-Fulda (Hahn 1954). " [77]

The pre-Bonifatian church

"The pre-Bonifatian church" should also be mentioned here. It says: "The construction work in the cathedral in Fulda in 1977 (installation of underfloor heating) gave us the opportunity to constantly observe the work. [...]

Immediately in front of the western end of the Sturmius Church, at a depth of 2.06 m, there was an excellent, concrete-hard floor. Vonderau had already found it and

---

[77] Roth, Wamers (Editor): Hessen im Frühmittelalter Archäologie und Kunst, S.302f.

thought it was a western crypt in front of the Sturmius church. In these areas, the floor is sunk into a wide shell limestone crib, so that up to 1 m high, neatly beveled walls indicate the limit. "

In addition to many other information, at the end it says: "The dimensions of the pre-monastery church are contemporary: the width of the nave outside 11.90 m and inside 10 m. Width of the sanctuary outside 10.50 m and inside 8.60 m may have been around 25 m (Hahn 1980). " [78]

The bridge

"The Fulda used to flow closer to the boundary of the Curtis and the following monastery. The distance was 60 to 70 m. Prehistoric finds show a ford a little above the confluence of the Waidesbach in the Fulda. But already around 300 AD there was a wooden bridge here. The dating is given by a Germanic foot vessel that was found on a broken compartment of the bridge. It was then replaced by the stone Long Bridge in the 9th century. The wooden bridge connected Eihloha-Fulda with the ridge trails, especially with the Untermain-Thuringia and Mittelmain-Leinetal connection (Vonderau 1931a). " [79]

The attachment

"The base zones of the western walls of the monastery should follow the old lines of the Curtis. This fortification has obviously taken over the Benedictine monastery. After a Hungarian invasion in 915 they were reinforced. [...] " [80]

---

[78] Roth, Wamers (Editor): Hessen im Frühmittelalter Archäologie und Kunst, S.303

[79] Roth, Wamers (Editor): Hessen im Frühmittelalter Archäologie und Kunst, S.303

[80] Roth, Wamers (Editor): Hessen im Frühmittelalter Archäologie und Kunst, S.304

Meaning of the Curtis Eihloha

Only the sentence should be mentioned here:
"It is not certain when the Curtis was destroyed by fire. It can be assumed that this happened occasionally during a military advance of the Saxons to the south in the time around 700." [81] The book continues with the chapter "The Sturmius Monastery".

Ludwig the Pious and his denarius in Fulda

In the subsection "Winkelbau" I quoted:
"On this wall there was a denarius of Louis the Pious [...], a further indication of a secondary use of this building in the monastery period."
If the time between September 1, 614 and August 31, 911 were fictitious, the question would arise what this coin is all about.
I can think of two ways to do this:
• The coin is a later counterfeit.
• The coin refers to a Merovingian Clovis, and the name is written in Latin on the coin. Would this be conceivable?

Brief conclusion from my side

I have the feeling that by the possible phantom time a) the achievements of the Romans are diminished, b) the Germanic nobility with Charlemagne seems exaggeratedly powerful, c) genealogy research into the Roman period is impossible from the start.

---

[81] Roth, Wamers (Editor): Hessen im Frühmittelalter Archäologie und Kunst, S.304

Reference to an illustration

Sandstone heads, Ottonian monk's head (10th century),
Fulda
In: Christoph Nicht, Das Dommuseum Fulda, Verlag
Parzeller, 1996, S.23
In: Dommuseum Fulda, Kurzführer durch die Ausstellung,
S.2 (ca. Jahr 2000)

Could that be Abbot Hadamar?
There are many different possibilities.

My two german written books used

Die verfälschte Antike (May 2013)
Dr. Illig & Angriff des Islam auf Rom bereits 337 n.Chr.
ISBN 978-3-7322-0769-5

Abt Hadamar bis Rose Hattemer (Nov 2019)
ISBN 978-3-7481-4608-7

Web pages on annual rings, astronomy, Islam

http://www.adalbert-feltz.at/2017/03/23/die-realitaet-
der-mittelalterlichen-phantomzeit-und-ihre-konsequenzen/

https://docplayer.org/165178309-H-e-korth-der-groesste-
irrtum-der-weltgeschichte.html

References (First Part)

Propyläen Weltgeschichte
Eine Universalgeschichte
Herausgeber: Golo Mann & Alfred Heuß
Propyläen Verlag Berlin
Ullstein GmbH Verlage Frankfurt am Main
Copyright im Jahr 1991

Der Grosse Ploetz
Die Daten-Enzyklopädie der Weltgeschichte
32.Auflage
Herder Verlag, Freiburg
Jahr 1998

Das Erfundene Mittelalter
Die größte Zeitfälschung der Geschichte
Heribert Illig
ECON-Verlag GmbH, Düsseldorf und München
3. Auflage 1997

Wer hat an der Uhr gedreht
Wie 300 Jahre Mittelalter erfunden wurden
Heribert Illig
3. Auflage 2000
ECON Ullstein List Verlag GmbH & Co. KG, München

Im Glanze Allahs
Die arabische Kulturwelt und Europa
Eberhard Serauky
Jahr 2004
be.bra verlag GmbH, Berlin-Brandenburg

Der Spiegel
Geschichte
Persien
Supermacht der Antike

Gottesstaat der Mullahs
Nr.2 / Jahr 2010
Spiegel-Verlag Rudolf Augstein GmbH & Co.KG, Hamburg

dtv-Atlas zur Weltgeschichte Band 1v2
Von den Anfängen bis zur Französischen Revolution
17. Auflage, Jahr 1981
Deutscher Taschenbuch-Verlag, München

Geschichtsatlas
Völker, Staaten und Kulturen
Georg Westermann Verlag, Braunschweig
Jahr 1976

Byzanz
John Haldon
Geschichte und Kultur eines Jahrtausends
Deutsche Übersetzung
Patmos Verlag GmbH & Co.KG, Düsseldorf
2007

Chronik der Deutschen
Chronik-Verlag, Dortmund, 1983

Das antike Persien
Josef Wiesehöfer
Von 550 v.Chr. bis 650 n.Chr.
Artemis und Winkler Verlag, Zürich und München, 1993

Das frühe Persien
Geschichte eines antiken Weltreichs
Josef Wiesehöfer
C.H. Beck'sche Verlagsbuchhandlung, München, 1999

Phänomen Zeit
Die unsichtbare kosmische Macht
Stratis Karamanolis

Neubiberg bei München, 1989
Elektra-Verlags GmbH

Irak
Sumerische Tempel, Babylons Paläste und heilige Stätten
des Islam im Zeitstromland
Wolfgang Göckel
DuMont Buchverlag, Köln, 2001

Iran
Mahmoud Rashad
DuMont Kunstreiseführer
3. Auflage, 2002

Iran
Claudia Stodte
Edition Temmen, Bremen, 1999

Iran
Reisehandbuch
Hans Berger
Conrad Stein Verlag GmbH, Welver
7. Auflage, 2005

Attila, der Hunnenkönig
Mann und Mythos
Patrick Howarth
Herder Verlag, Freiburg, Basel, Wien, 2001

Die Hunnen
Attila probt den Weltuntergang
Hermann Schreiber
ECON-Verlag, Wien, Düsseldorf, Neuauflage 1987

verschiedene PC.Software:
- Ermittlung Wochentag 614 911
- Ermittlung exakte Uhrzeit von Frühlingsanfang

Faszination Sonnenuhr
Zenkert, Arnold
Thun, Frankfurt am Main,
2. Auflage, 1995

Kosmos
Das Himmelsjahr 2002
2001, Franck-Kosmos
Verlags-GmbH & Co, Stuttgart
Thema. Tag- und Nachtgleiche

F.S. Sawelski,
Die Zeit und ihre Messung
Verlag Harri Deutsch, Thun & Frankfurt am Main, 1977

Hans-Ulrich Keller
Astrowissen (Zahlen, Daten, Fakten)
Franckh-Kosmos Verlags GmbH, Stuttgart, 1994

Lexikon der Astronomie
Steiger Verlag Augsburg, 1999
Weltbild Ratgeber Verlage GmbH & Co. KG

dtv-Atlas zur Astronomie
Joachim Herrmann
Deutscher Taschenbuch Verlag, München, 1973

Bertelsmann Lexikon Astronomie
Joachim Herrmann
Deutscher Taschenbuch Verlag, München, 1993
Bearbeitete, aktualisierte Auflage 1996

Schülerduden „Die Astronomie"
Wolfram Winnenburg
Bibliographisches Institut & F.A.Brockhaus AG, Mannheim,
1989

Das Lexikon der Astronomie
übersetzt aus dem Englischen von
The Astronomy Enzyclopaedia
Patrick Moore
Mitchell Beazley Publishers 1987
Herder Verlag, Freiburg im Breisgau, 1989

Einführung in die Astronomie
Wolfram Winnenburg
Bibliographisches Institut & F.A.Brockhaus AG, Mannheim,
1991

Die Merowinger und das Frankenreich
Eugen Ewig
4. Auflage, 2001
W. Kohlhammer GmbH, Stuttgart

Die Sonne
Der Stern, um den sich alles dreht
Richard Cohen
Arche-Verlag
Zürich, Hamburg
2012

Wunderwelt Wissen
Gruner & Jahr
Verlagsgruppe München
Artikel: Die geheimen Sternencodes der Majas
Januar 2013

Hörzu Wissen
Verlag Axel Springer
Die 13 größten Verschwörungstheorien der Weltgeschichte
Dez. 2012 / Jan. 2013

References (Second Part)

Beumann, Helmut, Die Ottonen, Verlag Kohlhammer, Stuttgart, 1987

Bischöfliches Dom- und Diözesanmuseum Mainz, Postkarte „Hattofenster, 1861 gefunden bei St. Mauritius, Mainz, um 900", Foto von Alberto Luisa, München, Brescia

Chronik der Deutschen, 1. Auflage, Chronik-Verlag Harenberg usw., Dortmund, 1983

Dehio, Georg und Gall, Ernst, Handbuch der Deutschen Kunstdenkmäler, Hessen, Deutscher Kunstverlag, München, Berlin, 1982

Fried, Johannes, Das Reich der Ottonen, in: Geschichte Deutschlands bis 1024, Band 1, Propyläen-Verlag, Berlin, 1994

Heinzelmann, Martin, Gregor von Tours (538-594), Zehn Bücher Geschichte, Wiss. Buchgesellschaft Darmstadt, 1994

Hiller, Helmut, Otto der Große und seine Zeit, List-Verlag, München, 1980

Illig, Heribert, Wer hat an der Uhr gedreht, ECON Taschenbuch Verlag, München, 3. Auflage, 2000

Leinweber, Josef, Die Fuldaer Äbte und Bischöfe, Verlag Josef Knecht, Frankfurt am Main, 1989

Ludowici, Babette, Frühmittelalterliche islamische Fayence aus Fulda, in: Germania, Jahrgang 72, Verlag Philipp von Zabern, Mainz, 1994

Nicht, Christoph, Das Dommuseum Fulda, Hrsg. Domkapitel Fulda, Verlag Parzeller, Fulda, 1996

Nitschke, August, Frühe christliche Reiche, in this: Die Ottonen, ein Herrscherhaus aus Sachsen, in: Golo Mann, Propyläen der Weltgeschichte, Band 5, S. 275-393, Ullstein-Verlag, Frankfurt am Main & Propyläen-Verlag, Berlin, 1991

Pauly-Wissowa, Realencyclopädie der classischen Alterstumswissenschaft, Reihe 1, 47 Halbbände, Reihe 2, 19 Halbbände, 15 Supplementbände, Stuttgart, München, 1893-1978

Roth, Helmut und Wamers, Egon (Hrsg.), Hessen im Frühmittelalter Archäologie und Kunst, Jan Thorbecke Verlag, Sigmaringen, 1984

Schmid, Karl, Die Klostergemeinschaft von Fulda im frühen Mittelalter, Band 1, Wilhelm Fink Verlag, München, 1978

Sturm, Erwin, Die Bau- und Kunstdenkmale der Stadt Fulda, Parzeller Verlag, Fulda, 1984

Vonderau, Joseph, Die Ausgrabungen am Dome zu Fulda in den Jahren 1908-1913, Veröffentlichung des Fuldaer Geschichtsvereins, Fulda, 1919

Vonderau, Joseph, Die Ausgrabungen am Dome zu Fulda in den Jahren 1919-1924, Veröffentlichung des Fuldaer Geschichtsvereins, Fulda, 1924

Wies, Ernst W., Otto der Große, Kämpfer und Beter, 2. Auflage, Verlag Bechtle, Esslingen, 1991

Translation mostly with Google Translator

With Deepl:
Beginnings of Islam: 300 years earlier? -- up to
Counter against phantom time
Blurring traces, e.g. beginning of the year -- up to
One repetition to deepen
Annual rings - no linearity at approx. 300 years– up to --
Sources in Persia
Ancient astronomer incapable AND brilliant?

It is possible that the translation from German to English is
incorrect in a few places.

Besides, something about two of my other books:

1) Update ROSE HATTEMER, founder private school, Paris:
Holger Schulz wrote to me, that she was born 1.5.1863 in
Paris and died there 10.11.1950. Her mother Louise born
Welter had been from Seltz (Alsace), but her father was not
an Hattemer/Alsace, but from Rheinhessen (Rhine-Hesse).
It was Philippe Antoine Hattemer, born 30.10.1830 in
Ockenheim, next to Gau-Algesheim, died 8.9.1874 in Paris.
He is the piano maker I mentioned in my book in 2019.
A brother of Rose Hattemer was director of HAPAG in Paris.
These persons are of Gau-Algesheim origin. They have to be
shifted from my book "Abt Hadamar bis Rose Hattemer" to
my book "Familien Hadamar bis Hattemer".

2) The first thought, that crossed my mind, when I saw the
"Rechtschreibreform" in 1996 was:
"I don't write any more letters after all."
("Ich schreibe doch nicht noch mehr Buchstaben!")
If you wish, look at my book from 2020:
Kürzere Wörter – spart 9% Typen

Thomas Hattemer, born 1967 in Bad Kreuznach, grew up in Pfaffen-Schwabenheim, graduated in 1994 with a diploma in physics in Mainz.